# Falling Away

*Falling Away*

# FALLING AWAY

By Fred DeRuvo

*Falling Away*

Copyright © 2013 by Study-Grow-Know Ministries

All rights reserved. Written permission must be secured from the publisher to use or reproduce any part of this book, except brief quotations in critical reviews or articles.

Published in Scotts Valley, California, by Adroit Publications
www.studygrowknow.com • www.studygrowknowblog.com

Unless otherwise noted, Scripture quotations taken from the New American Standard Bible®, Copyright © 1960, 1962, 1963, 1968, 1971, 1972, 1973, 1975, 1977, 1995 by The Lockman Foundation. Used by permission. (www.Lockman.org)

All Woodcuts used herein are in the Public Domain and free of copyright.

All Figure illustrations used in this book were created by the author and protected under copyright laws, © 2013.

Edited by: Hannah Brady

Cover Images: © 1xpert - Fotolia.com and © Les Cunliffe - Fotolia.com

Cover layout and design: Fred DeRuvo

**Library of Congress Cataloging-in-Publication Data**

DeRuvo, Fred, 1957 –

ISBN 0988183331
EAN-13 978-0-9881833-3-9

1. Religion – Religion / Religion, Politics & State

*"Let no one deceive you by any means; for that Day will not come unless the falling away comes first..."* – 2 Thessalonians 2:3

# Contents

| | | |
|---|---|---|
| Foreword | | vii |
| Chapter 1: | The Great Falling Away | 9 |
| Chapter 2: | When America Jumped the Shark | 17 |
| Chapter 3: | The '50s and '60s | 22 |
| Chapter 4: | Uninformed | 38 |
| Chapter 5: | Cultural Marxism | 46 |
| Chapter 6: | Racial Injustice | 63 |
| Chapter 7: | Subjective Virtue | 69 |
| Chapter 8: | Dumbing It Down | 77 |
| Chapter 9: | Politically Correct Christianity | 85 |
| Chapter 10: | Politically Correct Noah | 92 |
| Chapter 11: | Politically Correct Protesting | 99 |
| Chapter 12: | Political Correctness on Parade! | 107 |
| Chapter 13: | Political Correctness is (Not) Fabulous! | 113 |
| Chapter 14: | Critical Race Theory | 121 |
| Chapter 15: | Sound Political Theology | 129 |
| Chapter 16: | Fort Hood's Political Correctness | 137 |
| Chapter 17: | Politically Correct Ignorance | 144 |
| Chapter 18: | Racial Problems in the Big City | 152 |
| Chapter 19: | Does the End Justify the Means? | 159 |
| Chapter 20: | The "Victim" and the "Aggressor" | 166 |
| Chapter 21: | Only One Solution | 174 |
| Chapter 22: | Looking Ahead | 180 |

## Foreword

The Bible speaks of a "falling away" that will occur during the end times and it would happen *prior* to the revealing or appearance of the Antichrist ("man of sin"). Paul speaks of this in 2 Thessalonians 2:3.

Many have discussed and even debated the meaning of this "falling away." Some Bible translations use the phrase "the apostasy" or "the rebellion." At one point, I used to think that this falling away spoken of in the Bible referenced *professing* Christians falling away from the faith. In doing more research on the matter, while I still believe that this is *part* of what constitutes the falling away, I no longer believe that it is the *complete* aspect of this falling away.

I believe that this falling away not only encompasses those who *profess* to know Jesus as Savior and Lord, but speaks of society as a whole that, while at one time had evidenced some form of adherence to biblical values, has grown to a point of having nothing to do with God. In essence then, the falling away – to my way of thinking – speaks of a much larger scale moral failure that permeates society as a whole and references society's inability to maintain at least some semblance of *moral absolutes*.

I believe that this phenomenon began to take place on a large scale as the 1950s turned into the 1960s. There were a great many things happening in the world then and throughout the United States in particular. As society moved from one decade to the next, the changes that were taking place framed the way people thought, acted, and lived.

In fact, the change has been so dramatic that I believe it is impossible to go *backward*. It is, therefore, too late for society to return to a time of innocence and relative selflessness. Since things changed in the 1960s, people (and humanity as a whole) have become far more self-centered, rather than actively asking what they can do to *help* people improve by giving of themselves for that purpose.

While this book is *not* meant to be a detailed history of past decades, I have taken the time to highlight the events that I believe were catalysts in creating change within and throughout society. These changes have prompted us to become what is mirrored in civilization today.

In many ways, there is no going back. We have crossed the line and the structures, attitudes, and thinking that brought about this change have been in place for many generations. The changes themselves seemed to have become most obvious during the 1960s and '70s.

In another book I wrote – *Living in the Last Generation* – I discuss why I believe we are that last generation before the physical return of Jesus Christ. Those reasons are discussed from a biblical perspective, citing Matthew 24 as the main text.

In this book – *Falling Away* – I refer to the many secular changes throughout society that have created a new foundation upon which the world now moves, something that is seen as the *new* truth. One thing is important to remember, regardless of whether we are talking about biblical signs or secular changes: *God is fully in control.* He has never given up His sovereignty related to any portion of His Creation and never will.

What we view as human history is little more than seeing God's hand from *our* perspective, though usually ignoring the fact that God has been involved. I pray that before you finish this book, you would come to recognize that God is King. God alone is sovereign, fully in control of all outcomes in order that the perfection of His will might be brought to bear on this universe.

In some ways, we are all players in His pageant. By His grace, we choose the side we are on: Satan's or God's. I pray that you have made the correct choice.

*- Fred DeRuvo, April 2013*

# Chapter 1
# The Great Falling Away

This book is about the great falling away that the apostle Paul warns of in 2 Thessalonians 2. He indicated this would occur as the world approached the *end* of the End Times (the times that began with the life, death, and resurrection of Jesus). The world would essentially come to a point where it no longer wished to have anything to do with God and His standards.

I will admit that I used to think that phrase was fairly limited in scope, in that I felt Paul was mainly dealing with *Christendom* and the "falling away" that would occur within it from those who *profess* to be Christians but are not truly *authentic* Christians. These folks have not had the *spiritual transaction* that Jesus speaks of in John 3. It was there, in His conversation with Nicodemus, that Jesus pointed out that in order to gain eternal life, a person must be born again, or born from above.

This concept is certainly very important to grasp because in it, we find the very act and foundation that creates authentic Christianity within each true believer. Being a Christian is not simply following a set of rules, or even doing our best to love God above all things and our neighbors as we love ourselves. It is much more than that and I believe the truth is often missed by many today.

Certainly people like Brian McLaren, Rick Warren, Tony Campolo, and too many others to name here explain Christianity from a postmodern standpoint, often leaving out the very fact of what Jesus explained succinctly to Nicodemus. In order to gain eternal life, a person *must* be born again. That is the starting point. Our ability to love people – such as it is with a fallen nature – is *not* the start. The ability to truly love people comes *after* a person has been born again, not before.

Anyone can *appear* as though they love another person or people in general. The nature of such acts that *appear* loving can be so real that they even convince the person who is doing the alleged loving that they *are* real. God says our hearts are deceitfully wicked in Jeremiah 17:9. Who among us can actually know the true condition of the heart? Of course, God knows. Anything done in the strength of *self* (no matter how real it may appear) will burn up in judgment, but things done in God's strength will remain (cf. 1 Corinthians 3:12-13).

As much as I believe that there is a problem within Christendom occurring these days – with many falling away from the truth – I no longer see that as the sole concern of Paul. It is *part* of it, yes, but not all of it.

Ever since I published a book called *The Anti-Supernatural Bias of Ex-Christians* back in 2009, I have realized that there is a growing group of people who firmly believe themselves to have *been* Christian (authentically) yet have walked away from the faith and no longer consider themselves to be Christian. In fact, many have settled in nicely (it would seem) under the category of either atheist or agnostic, but mostly atheist. This burgeoning group of individuals is certainly part of what the apostle Paul was referring to when he penned the words of 2 Thessalonians 2 a few thousand years ago.

My question is, how is it possible for a person who has allegedly become born again to then become "unborn again"? How is that possible? Once a person is born, they cannot be unborn. Death is not being unborn. It is the cessation of the life that once existed. A person who is truly born again, or born from above, remains that for all eternity.

I believe Paul was implying something far wider in scope than simply talking about those who professed to be Christians and then walked away completely. I now believe he was talking about a huge cultural shift that would take place worldwide in the End Times. I especially believe this will occur in places like America where the founding documents of our country referenced God, understood that He exists as Creator, and in fact laid the foundation for this country solidly upon biblical principles. While this does not presuppose a covenant with God, the clear reality is that His truth was included in the process of creating America.

Unfortunately, something else has clearly taken over America, pushing it from its biblical moorings to something that is tragically opposed to it. That something is cultural Marxism. Cultural Marxism is different from economic Marxism. In cultural Marxism, the general idea is to recreate a culture with principles that are essentially opposed to biblical standards.

William S. Lind is a well-known individual who has spoken a good deal about this phenomenon, and his many writings have explained it more than satisfactorily. *"Cultural Marxism is a branch of western Marxism, different from the Marxism-Leninism of the old Soviet Union. It is commonly known as 'multiculturalism' or, less formally, Political Correctness. From its beginning, the promoters of cultural Marxism have known they could be more effective if they concealed the Marxist nature of their work, hence the use of terms such as 'multiculturalism'."*[1]

In short, cultural Marxism opposes anything and everything that is traditional in scope and based on biblical tenets. For instance, in the Bible, marriage is between one man and one woman. Opposing that means pushing for gay and lesbian rights, which allows two men or two women to marry one another, elevating that union to the same standard as two members of the opposite sex marrying.

Whereas the Bible sees the male as the spiritual head of the home, cultural Marxism seeks to reverse roles. Anything that attacks biblical mandates and tenets is seen as the new normal, while biblical mandates become antiquated and based on "hatred." Therefore, those who continue to observe them are "haters" themselves. This, of course, leads to speech codes and addresses the issue of hate speech. So, concluding that the Bible prohibits homosexual unions is tantamount to "hate speech" and will one day be illegal in the United States, as it currently is in the UK and other places.

Essentially then, one of the foundational goals of cultural Marxism is to eradicate Christianity in the West. This has been in the works since World War I. Has it been a conspiracy, where human beings have gathered together for the purpose of trying to accomplish this? I have no idea, but I do know that from the *spiritual* realm, Satan has

---

[1] http://www.marylandthursdaymeeting.com/Archives/SpecialWebDocuments/Cultural.Marxism.htm

done everything he can to turn things upside down in society so that we have come to a point where evil is called good and good is called evil.

If you consider the fact that if this has been in the works since WWI, it is not at all difficult to see that cultural Marxism went mainstream in the 1960s. If we consider all that took place during that decade alone, it becomes easy to see how society has increasingly opposed anything biblical.

In the 1960s, we took God, His Word, and prayer out of the public schools. In the 1970s, we made it legal to kill unborn children. Sadly, there are many so-called Christians who have little to no problem with abortion and because of it many can easily vote for a pro-abortion political candidate.

So in the space of just over ten years, we passed laws that literally abandoned God and several of the Ten Commandments, including the sixth: thou shalt not kill. Whatever America's foundation was built on, we collectively voted to overturn it in the '60s and '70s.

Since that time, what has been the result? Crime has gone up, families have been split apart, and children have experienced problems and difficulties like ADHD, depression, and a host of mental ailments that are coming home to roost.

Never fear though, because atheists and humanists alike have been trying ever since to replace God, His Word, and prayer with something else entirely. It has many names, depending upon the branch of society through which it has been introduced: New Age, Reiki, mindfulness, Humanistic Psychology, Darwinism, Ecumenism, Socialism, Diversity Training, Relativism, political correctness, Globalism, speech codes, New Media, Mainstream (or Mainline) Christianity, Christian Cultural Marxism, Postmodernism, Emergent Church, Frankfurt School, and more.

The saddest part, of course, is that nothing can replace God: absolutely nothing. He is the way, the truth, and the life (John 14:6). He is not "a" way, "a" truth, or "a" life. Yet Satan continues to lie to the world, telling society that we can find peace with God and happiness within ourselves through something *other* than God. This is essentially the same lie he used against Adam and Eve.

One of the big new things making its way into schools is called Mindfulness, or Mindfulness of Purpose. It is a way of thinking that teaches students (and educators) how to help themselves make good decisions. Ultimately, what is fascinating about it is that it is based directly on the eight main tenets of Buddhism. Reiki, which is growing in usage in many health clinics, is also based on Buddhist techniques. Again, I will have far more detail in my upcoming book.

When we take the time to look squarely in the face of the society in which we now live, it becomes clear that because we have kicked God out of schools and out of virtually every place in society except houses of worship, society has failed and will continue to fail. The devolution is nearly complete.

The great falling away has taken and will continue to take place globally. It's not just the fact that tremendous numbers of people who have previously professed to be Christian are moving away from Christianity. More to the point is the fact that all of society is moving away from any desire to even know God, just as society has done previously, as described by Paul in Romans 1.

Yet we have what are known as "mega-churches" where thousands of people gather together to "worship" God. How do we account for that? The same apostle Paul who speaks of the great falling away also tells us of the growing desire of people to have their ears tickled (2 Timothy 4:3). This, of course, is when a person only wants to hear things that make him feel good about himself, others, and life in general. Unfortunately, there are way too many preachers who are far more inclined to tell people what they want to hear as opposed to what God wants them to know.

Society is falling away. It has been doing it for some time and it will continue to do so. People have been arrested for kneeling in prayer in front of the White House or the building that houses the Supreme Court. This happened in 2012 several times.[2]

In the end, cultural Marxism attacks the very fundamental rights of American citizens as guaranteed by the Constitution and Bill of Rights. Through speech codes, political correctness, and multiculturalism, policy and even laws are passed denoting when something is considered to be "hate" speech. This is an abrogation of the First Amendment. Is it good when people use terms that offend others? Of course not, but to make laws or policy against it is absurd. It simply whittles away at our rights. Let's not even talk about who decides what constitutes "hate speech."

Cultural Marxism encourages people to think that laws must be enacted for the safety of all people but too often wind up simply reducing the rights of the law-abiding citizen. Such is the case with respect to the fervor over the Second Amendment. All people should be willing to give up gun rights so that everyone will be "safer," yet there is no way to ensure that criminals would ever comply. This is cultural Marxism because it tries to make guns – in this case – the bad guy, when the bad guy is still the person who wields the gun and uses it for criminal activity. Cultural Marxism can do nothing about that bad guy.

Yes, there is a falling away that has been at work within Christendom, but there is also a falling away from any semblance of biblical standards in society as a whole. This falling away is described as a "rebellion" by Paul in the English Standard Version of 2 Thessaloni-

---

[2] http://www.lifesitenews.com/news/54-arrested-so-far-in-white-house-vigil-for-religious-liberty/

ans 2:3. It is called the "apostasy" in the New American Standard Version, and the phrase "people rise up against God" is used in the New International Version. The sense here is that this will occur throughout society, including Christendom.

The further people go from God and the more they want no part of Him, the greater will their rebellion be. Their attitudes will mirror their hearts. They will no longer serve anything but themselves.

So, where does that leave society? For godless people, it leaves them without hope. However, that may wind up being a good place for many, because in their hopelessness and despair, God may yet open their eyes so that they can see the truth. He may also use those of us who already know Him to help them open their eyes. Because of that, we always need to be prepared to give an answer for the hope that we have in Christ Jesus (cf. 1 Peter 3:15). As long as a person has breath, salvation is available.

For Christians, we know that even though society will ultimately fail and crumble, Jesus will be victorious. What is happening in society now will only serve to ultimately give way to His rule. It is that we look forward to and it is why we pray, "Come quickly, Lord Jesus!"

## Chapter 2
# When America Jumped the Shark

It's very much like the parable told of the frog that is placed in a pot of cold water on a stove. Heat is applied very slowly to the pot. Over time, the frog simply boils to death because it had no real ability to discern that the water was going from cold, to hot, to boiling because the process happened so slowly.

There seem to be two types of changes that take place in society. First, we have the change that is very slow and incremental. This type of change is not really noticed by most until all of a sudden one day the majority of people realize what has occurred. Second, we have change that literally *overwhelms* society, creating massive change overnight. I believe both of these things have been brought to bear on society.

Just a quick look at technology tells us how far (and how fast) we have come from where we were, not really that long ago. It was actually only back in the 1980s when personal computers (PCs) really came to the fore. Yes, they existed prior to that time, but they were not generally available to the public due to excessive cost.

Early in the 1980s, PCs became much more available because components became less expensive. In fact, many of those computers then could be connected to a TV. Games and accessories for them were fairly inexpensive as well due to the lack of high-quality graphics. Over time, costs have increased for software (normally due to programming hours/labor), while parts and accessories for computers themselves have declined.

But if we consider just how far computers have come in the space of just under 30 years, it is astounding. During the 1980s, I worked at Radio Shack, and the computers sold then were considered to be state of the art. Games were pretty much text-based and in order to play them, the game (usually on a cassette tape) was inserted into a tape player and the cassette player itself was attached to the computer console.

Information from the computer was usually saved on the large 5¼" floppy disk (or built-in hard disk drive). Of course, these were eventually replaced with the smaller 3½" disks, which also held more information. These were all but fully replaced with CDs and USB thumb drives not too many years later.

The same thing has happened with cell phones. The first ones that were commercially available *and* fairly affordable looked like household phones (the *old* kind from the 1950s and '60s). I recall buying one of those "new" cell phones as a Christmas present for my wife one year. It came in a bag that resembled a large purse. The part of the phone that you listened to and spoke through was connected to the base of the cell phone via a coiled cord. If memory serves, the cost of a call was seventy-five cents per minute at that time, so we only used it for emergencies.

Now, several decades later, phones easily fit into our pockets (or purses) and are essentially mini-computers with phone capabilities. Most cell phone providers offer unlimited phone calls and texting for one monthly fee.

This same technology has improved automobiles and many other things in society. These types of changes are remarkable, and it reminds me of Daniel 12:4 where, after Daniel is told to seal up the vision until the end times, he is told *"many will go back and forth, and knowledge will increase."*

The idea here is that people will be on a serious quest for knowledge. They won't be able to get enough. They will run here and there trying to learn as much as possible. While this *may* be referencing knowledge in the religious realm, it could also apply to the areas of technology that continue to grow and change.

The remarkable thing is that just when we think that technology cannot go any further, something is created that allows just that to happen. We are left wondering, what change will take place next? What will the next greatest invention be for society?

The example of the speed with which technological changes push society in one direction or another is easy to see and understand (even if we do not fully understand the actual technology itself). It takes place all around us and we see the results and usage of that technology on a daily basis.

Even though the individual changes in society are often clearly seen, what is sometimes *not* seen as readily is the spiritual and even unintended results of those societal changes. Often, the types of changes I'm referring to (which we explore in more depth as we progress through this book) resonate throughout society to create additional changes that were not necessarily intended when the first change took place.

For instance, it can be argued that *abortion* has played a very key role in *changing* the way people think about life in general. It was first declared that by keeping abortion *illegal*, women were dying unnecessarily in what were termed "back alley" abortion clinics. These clandestine facilities were dirty, unsafe, and generally dreaded.

Making abortion legal – it was said – would mean that those who felt there was no other choice than to have an abortion would be *safer* during the procedure. Eventually, because of Norma L. McCorvey (who was pregnant with her third child at the time), the entire subject of abortion headed to the Supreme Court. The court ruled that abortion was a fundamental right and from that time (1973) through today, abortions have taken place in the United States on a daily basis. Roughly 3,800 unborn children are killed every day in America.

By the end of 2011, there were 54,559,615 abortions that had occurred in abortion clinics throughout America.[3] In 1973, there were just fewer than 80,000 abortions that took place. At its highest point, in 1990, abortions rose to just over 1.6 million, leveling off to just over 1.2 million abortions in 2011.[4]

So, is 1973 then the time when America jumped the shark morally? In my opinion, *no*. That took place even *prior* to the abortion battle that culminated with the Supreme Court's ruling in favor of it, though the abortion situation here in America did not help. So when then? Events occurred prior to Roe v. Wade that made it acceptable in society to allow and accept as right the slaughtering of unborn children.

---

[3] http://www.mccl.org/us-abortion-stats.html (February 22, 2013)
[4] Ibid

Did America jump the shark when the Supreme Court pushed God, the Ten Commandments, and prayer out of public schools?

What we need to do is look closely at the events that have occurred in America and that have reduced this nation's quality of life. Was it the decision on abortion, the elimination of the Ten Commandments, or something else altogether that caused America to begin to lose its moral high ground?

Let's take some time to go back through the numerous decades of America's past to see what we can learn. The answer may surprise you.

## Chapter 3
# The '50s and the '60s

Example of artwork for Coca-Cola ad from the 1960s
by Pete Hawley

In many ways, the decade of the 1950s in America highlighted a society that, by and large, was naïve in their beliefs. We were "cool," things were "neato," and life was just "swell."

This is not to say that Americans were stupid. Far from it. Stupidity is not the same as naiveté. At the time, Americans generally believed their government. They also believed they had a lot to look forward to in life.

It is important to point out, though, that no period of time in America (or any other nation) was perfect. There were problems in the

1950s; however, there was almost an idyllic outlook on life that made people believe that the best was yet to come. Let's take a few moments to look at some of the highlights of that period of time, along with the overall attitudes that permeated society then.

World War II had just recently ended (1945) and hundreds of thousands of servicemen were returning to the United States to pick up life where they had left it. They wanted jobs, their own families, and the good things life had to offer. They had seen enough death and destruction to last a lifetime and wanted to move on.

They returned as heroes to a land that, for all practical purposes, was undiscovered territory. There was so much that was wide open to them and they wanted to take advantage of it.

Here are a few important facts to know about the decade of the **1950s**:

- *Population: 151,684,000 (U.S. Dept. of Commerce, Bureau of the Census)*
- *Unemployed: 3,288,000*
- *Life expectancy: women 71.1, men 65.6*
- *Car Sales: 6,665,800*
- *Average Salary: $2,992*
- *Labor Force male/female: 5/2*
- *Cost of a loaf of bread: $0.14*
- *Bomb shelter plans, like the government pamphlet You Can Survive, become widely available*[5]

These are interesting facts, but you might also be interested to know that gas then cost twenty cents per gallon, mailing a First Class letter cost three cents, an average home would set you back about $18,000,

---

[5] http://kclibrary.lonestar.edu/decade50.html (February 22, 2013)

and a T-bone steak could be purchased for ninety-five cents per pound.[6]

Of course, based on the average salary noted above, your money seemed to go much further than it does today because of inflation as well as the additional taxes most of us pay to the government. The 1950s proved to be a time of real prosperity for most Americans.

Besides these things, what were the 1950s like for the average American? Well, life was generally presented as cheerful, for lack of a better word, on television, a relatively new medium.

Shows like *Lassie*, *Rin-Tin-Tin*, *Flipper*, *The Virginian*, Disney's *Zorro*, *I Remember Mama*, *I Love Lucy*, *The Dick Van Dyke Show*, and many others reflected a real positive outlook for Americans. Though these shows dealt with problems, they always worked themselves out during the space of a particular episode.

These TV shows, along with many others, always portrayed the good guys as distinct from the bad guys. We knew who to root for and had no trouble discerning the good from the bad. There was always a general theme that was clearly morally upright, allowing Americans to use TV as teachable moments for children, or at least not have to worry about the messages children received from TV programming.

Even though television had been around in the United States since the 1920s, it wasn't until the mid-to-late 1940s that TV started to take off, and by the 1950s, millions of American households had at least one television set. Much of TV was live then, like *The Jackie Gleason Show*, as well as a good amount of children's programming.

It makes sense that since television was a relatively new medium, programming departments and stations were very careful and selective about what they showed on TV. Nothing was inordinate or

---

[6] http://www.loti.com/bargain_price.htm (February 22, 2013)

truly suggestive. There were plenty of rules that actors had to abide by, such as when a married couple was in bed, one of the performers had to have at least one foot on the floor.

In many cases, husband and wife slept in separate beds, like Rob and Laura Petrie on *The Dick Van Dyke Show*. This did not reflect real life, but it certainly made for much more comfortable viewing by families with children. However, over time, as we know, television began pushing the envelope, and once the moral walls started to come down, the flood gates opened.

During the 1950s, Americans also had a number of men that they respected greatly as presidents. These men – Harry S. Truman and later Dwight D. Eisenhower – appeared to stand heads above others for their integrity. Behind closed doors, this may not have always been the case, but as far as the person they portrayed to the public, their veracity was in tact.

People by and large were also very patriotic during this time period, which again makes sense if we consider that this time period follows the victories of WWII in chasing down Hitler's Third Reich. When the world realized the extent to which Hitler's regime had attempted to completely obliterate all people of Jewish descent, countries like America were looked upon as true heroes in the world. It was this type of pride that carried this country forward.

It was also this type of patriotism that caused our country – in large measure – to support the actions of Harry Truman. He was responsible for giving the go-ahead on the production of the hydrogen bomb and sent Air Force and Navy troops to Korea.

Of course, on the heels of WWII, people were (rightly) concerned about the infiltration of Communists into American society. While things may have become a bit overblown via the efforts of Sen. McCarthy, many believe that he was correct in his assumptions.

It is interesting to note that during that time period (1954 and following), Communists were identified and rooted out. Today, they are *embraced*. Communism hasn't *improved*, so what has changed? Obviously, it is the way people look at Communists today. Are they really a threat anymore? Doesn't our government talk *to* and connect *with* Russian leaders like Putin and Medvedev? What's the worry, many say? They argue the paranoia needs to stop.

The worry of course is that the same ideological outlook that has governed Communist nations in the 1950s governs these nations today. Nothing has really changed in the way Communists *think*. Times have changed, and in large part the way people see Communists has changed. They are no longer considered to be a threat to the American way of life because the American way of life has changed so drastically.

Consider the TV show *Happy Days* and how it reflected the way people were during the 1950s. While it wasn't all fun and games and cheerful smiles, the truth of the matter is that in many ways the 1950s *were* pleasant. However, as America moved toward the 1960s, attitudes did change. Questioning authority began in earnest and a form of revolt started to take place, especially among the young people of the 1950s.

*"America had just begun her recovery from World War II, when suddenly the Korean Conflict developed. The USSR became a major enemy in the Cold War. Senator Joseph McCarthy claimed to know that Communists had infiltrated the United States government at the highest levels. Americans were feeling a sense of national anxiety. Was America the greatest country in the world? Was life in America the best it had ever been? As the decade passed, literature reflected the*

*conflict of self-satisfaction with '50s Happy Days and cultural self-doubt about conformity and the true worth of American values."*[7]

As we move from the 1950s into the 1960s, we have to wonder what happened. What caused the transformation in society that formed the attitudes and actions that were so prevalent in the 1960s, and what effect did those attitudes and actions have on society at large?

## The 1960s

A great many things took place in the 1960s, creating major change throughout society, and, in the opinion of this author, not many of them were *good*. *"It was an era where America shifted from optimism to disillusionment, from blind acceptance to distrust. In ten short years, 'My country, right or wrong' morphed into 'Question authority'. It was a time of violent confrontation, with the civil rights movement and youth culture demanding equity when the war in Southeast Asia put civil loyalty to the test. The media reflected that confusion, with music in particular serving as a means of expression that heretofore did not exist."*[8]

Whatever we think about the 1960s, it should be agreed that there was a tremendous amount of adjustment that occurred throughout the world and certainly throughout the United States. The changes were obvious and often tumultuous.

In many ways, music dominated the world then. It created fashion as well as attitudes. It led the way for a generation of young people who were looking for their own pied piper. Music spoke *for* them. While at least some of the music was to some extent innocuous, at least at the start, it wasn't long before that gave way to music that was extremely political in nature.

---

[7] http://kclibrary.lonestar.edu/decade50.html (February 22, 2013)
[8] http://www.americanhitnetwork.com/ahn/decade-overview.cfm/decade/1960 (2/23/2013)

What had been a patriotic stand with respect to war and those who fought in it in the 1950s became a literal loathing of anything to do with war in the 1960s. Young people wanted love and peace, not war and death. This burgeoning attitude became the stuff songs were made of that carried a generation of young people into a culture of drugs, rebellion, and complete hatred of what came to be known as the "establishment."

For America especially, the 1960s became the backdrop of the counter-culture revolution of young people trying to remake America into something with which *they* could connect. It is easy to agree with one writer who stated, "*the 1960s remains the most consequential and controversial decade of the twentieth century. It would dawn bright with hope and idealism, see the liberal state attain its mightiest reforms and reach, and end in discord and disillusionment.*"[9]

I would go so far as to say that Satan, and the powers of darkness that serve him to this day from the spiritual realm, made one of his biggest pushes for social instability leading to change in the 1960s. The drive for societal change was so great that it really was impossible for society to resist. Transformation did come to America and in many ways, because of that, the fabric of American culture changed *forever*. Since then, modifications have continued until we are where we are today, fully able to agree with Isaiah that there are many in society who tell us that *evil is good* and *good is evil* (cf. Isaiah 5:20).

It seems clear enough that because of the relative prosperity of the late 1950s, people were able to reach for and take hold of what they believed was their portion of the American dream. It was there in plenty.

As GI's returned home from the war, jobs awaited them. They not only had jobs, but because of those jobs, along with the GI Bills that

---

[9] http://www.gilderlehrman.org/history-by-era/1945-present/sixties (02/23/2013)

gave breaks for further education as well as other perks to service personnel, ex-military personnel were now able to not only afford to buy their own home, but they could do so in the *suburbs*. Because of that, many families said good-bye to the lifestyle of the crowded, noisy cities and headed out to areas away from city life, but still close enough to drive into the city as needed.

In the suburbs, where people were able to stretch their wings, so to speak, homes were relatively affordable and even provided space for the kids to grow up and play in comparative safety, unlike the crowded conditions of the cities. The population in America at that time swelled, with approximately 70 million became teenagers and young adults during the '60s.[10]

While many of these things were good for Americans and for families, America was still suffocating from the unhealthy attitudes of racism. Beyond this, the general conservatism of the 1950s was being roundly rejected by many youths of the '60s. These wanted to make a name for themselves by creating their own generation that did *not* resemble that of their parents.

*"During the sixties, college campuses became centers of debate and scenes of protest more than ever before. Great numbers… of young adults, baby boomers, reaching military draft age (selective service) and not yet voting age (minimum voting age did not become 18 until 1971), caused a struggle which played out on many campuses as the country became more involved…in the Vietnam War. The generation gap became a growing phenomenon."*[11]

It was this juxtaposition of freedom to move with the inability to rise above racial tensions and war that created situations on many college campuses that brought students in direct conflict with authorities. Students saw the injustices and wanted them changed. The old

---

[10] http://kclibrary.lonestar.edu/decade60.html (02/23/2013)
[11] Ibid

guard – the established political pillars of society – did not want things to be changed and stood in the way. This was a recipe for disaster. It was also the obvious beginnings of cultural Marxism among the young.

*"During the 1960s, young Americans on and off campuses challenged conventional lifestyles and institutions. They protested the materialism, consumerism, and mania for success that drove American society. They urged people to explore alternative patterns of work and domesticity. They challenged traditions surrounding sex and marriage. And they argued that all paths to deeper fulfillment, even those involving illicit drugs, could be justified. They believed they were creating a new America."*[12]

It was, of course, during the 1960s that Vietnam came to the fore for America. Even though the Vietnam conflict began years earlier, it really was not until the early 1960s that American troops on the ground entered the conflict. Even larger amounts of combat troops were deployed to Vietnam in 1965.

It is necessary to remember that WWII ended in the late 1940s and America was ready for a break from war and fighting. With the escalation of conflict in Vietnam, many young men balked at the idea of heading overseas to fight in another foreign altercation that seemed to have nothing to do with America.

To make matters worse, when the military men from Vietnam returned to America from Vietnam, they were treated with disdain, as if fighting in that conflict had been their idea. They had been drafted and did what they believed was the correct thing to do, but the majority of America's young people did not see it that way and voiced their dissent.

---

[12] http://www.shmoop.com/1960s/summary.html (02/23/2013)

So with Americans sick of war, trouble brewed at home. Students from campuses like Berkeley, CA began to protest the war. Demonstrations soon caught on across the nation.

There are many individuals whose names are well known for their connection to the turmoil of the 1960s. Aside from the numerous leaders within the Civil Rights Movement and others who led the anti-Vietnam effort, one well-known individual was a man known as Dr. Spock. Spock was a pediatrician who attempted to psychoanalyze children to determine how to best meet their needs. He was also a vocal opponent of the Vietnam War.

In the 1950s, the mantra that children should essentially be seen and not heard still prevailed. If children got out of line, they should be physically punished via spankings. Spock came along and engendered more of a *complimentary* role with children. Because of this (and his political positions), some accused him of *pandering* to children, which, they charged, spoiled them.

So permissive was Spock and his ideas that he was blamed for a plethora of things within society. *"Dr. Spock came under fire for this political activism. Critics branded him the 'father of permissiveness' and said he was responsible for a 'Spock-marked generation of hippies.' In the 1960s, Vice President Agnew, Chicago Mayor Richard Daley, and New York Methodist Episcopal minister Norman Vincent Peale publicly attacked Spock, arguing that his methods of bringing up children had caused a 'breakdown in discipline and a collapse of conventional morality.' From his pulpit, Peale preached, 'And now Spock is out in the mobs, leading the permissive babies raised on his undisciplined teaching.'"*[13]

So, we can see that things were not well in the decade of the '60s. With the Vietnam War heating up (with American troops sent to join

---

[13] http://www.freerepublic.com/focus/f-chat/1796388/posts (02/23/2013)

the fray), the Civil Rights Movement gaining momentum led by the charismatic figure of Dr. Martin Luther King, Jr., and children being catered to by parents who bought (and agreed with) Dr. Spock's book (to the tune of 750,000 copies sold within six years of its publication[14]), society was going through major changes. There was no stopping it at all.

Couple this with the fact that during the war years of WWII, while men fought in the war overseas, many women took factory jobs and did so for two reasons. First, they were needed because of the absence of men. Someone was needed to help create the products that the American military and consumers needed. Second, the women needed to do something to bring in more money to support their families while the chief breadwinner was overseas fighting in the war.

With the end of WWII, many women were forced to give up their jobs so that returning GI's could have jobs. Yet many of these same women had grown accustomed to working outside the home and earning their own money. Going back to the "kitchen" was now no longer something that suited them. They liked what they had when they had earned their own paycheck, and many were loath to part with it.

This created another form of tension in which women that had a taste of the benefits of earning a paycheck wanted to continue that practice. So we began to see households that moved away from the *"Ozzie & Harriet"* or *"Father Knows Best"* families, where the father left for work each day while the mother remained home and took care of the responsibilities of the household.

What this also meant was that young people were on their own more often because of the absence of both parents, who had jobs in the workforce. This caused a lack of supervision as well as forced chil-

---

[14] http://www.freerepublic.com/focus/f-chat/1796388/posts (02/23/2013)

dren to learn to take care of themselves. It also meant that the lack of supervision created situations in which these young children had more freedom than they were generally prepared to handle. It was this type of freedom that created a generation of children who – as they got older – came to rely on themselves a great deal more to make their own decisions.

These decisions often included illicit drug use and sexual experimentation. With both parents away from the home after the kids got home from school, they were effectively on their own to do what parents hoped would be responsible decision-making. All too often, though, the decisions made were *not* responsible and were in fact detrimental.

It's almost as if Satan planned it this way. The information about a group known by its various names – the global elite, the elite, the Illuminati, the Bilderbergers, etc. – has taught me that most (possibly all) wars have been created by factions of the global elite (GE).

You might ask why the GE would work to *create* wars. It's done for a variety of reasons. Of course, the most important reason is twofold: to gain as much wealth as possible through the sales of ammunitions and other needed supplies for the war movement through companies owned by the GE, and also to keep society *on edge*. A society that is always concerned about what might happen if this war or that one breaks out is easier to manipulate than a society that is at peace due to a lack of concern about potential war.

Peace means enjoying life, raising a family, and benefitting from the good things that life has to offer. Peace means growing old gracefully while watching your children grow, marry, and have children of their own.

Wars and rumors of wars disrupt that peace. People act differently when they are in the midst of a war or when they think one might occur. It is this author's belief that the GE works diligently to *create* flux in society in a variety of ways and wars and rumors of wars are one of the best ways to achieve societal change and breakdown.

So, in a very real way, Satan *has* planned things this way so that wars always appear to be on the horizon. I believe he does this through the GE: hand-picked people and families that he has raised up, blessed with tremendous wealth, and has placed at the helm of his physical worldly kingdom for now. Together, they work toward the day when they believe they will welcome *The Christ* (of the New Age), who will guide and direct this world toward true global peace.

Daniel 9 speaks of wars and desolations unto the end (Daniel 9:27) and Jesus speaks of wars and rumors of wars in His Olivet Discourse of Matthew 24, Mark 13, and Luke 21. Wars keep people and governments off balance.

In order to help get this world to that point though, society needs to be in a place where it realizes that someone needs to arrive who will have the superior (and supernatural) intelligence to create true global peace. By keeping wars and rumors of wars (along with an increase in violence in society) on the front burner, the belief is that more and more people will call for the need for peace. They will want to work toward it and even such things as banning guns in society will be seen as necessary as just one means of reducing violence so that real peace can be achieved (as we are hearing today).

It is really impossible to look at society solely from the human perspective, as if humankind is the one (and only one) that has made decisions for change. The Bible tells us in numerous places that Satan is the god of this world (cf. 2 Corinthians 4:4) and ruler of the air above the earth (cf. Ephesians 2:2). The forces that exist in the spiritual realm work to bring Satan's goals to fruition. These forces exert energy on people in society to bring about these changes. People are the tools used to foster change.

We learn from the book of Job alone that Satan has tremendous power, though his power is always kept in check by God Himself. With Job, Satan wanted to prove to God that Job would not remain faithful when the going got tough. Satan's larger goal is to overthrow God, though ultimately any and all of Satan's efforts simply play into God's hands, bringing about God's purposes.

So when we look at the 1950s, '60s, '70s, or later, we should look at the actual things that caused change within society, the things we can see. But we should also be aware of the fact that those changes were stimulated by Satan and his powers of darkness in order to get this world to a point where a one-world, global government will prevail. This is what the Bible tells us will happen: that a final world empire will emerge and will be led by an individual Paul calls the "man of sin" (cf. 2 Thessalonians 2).

So again, there are two parts to the picture that we must always keep in mind: the *secular* portion where we actually *see* the changes that occur in society because of the events that promoted those changes, and the *spiritual* aspect of these changes that originate in the spiritual realm but that we are unable to see.

As the 1960s rolled on, things became severely inane, insane, and more inappropriate. But this is what many in that decade were hoping to achieve. The crazier and more outlandish it was, the more they wanted to do it because they felt that this was necessary in order to first, shock society into realizing what was wrong (according to them) and second, to create the change they felt was necessary in order to "save America."

We've all heard the expression, "*peace, love, dope!*" which, in three words, encapsulated the goals of the younger generation growing up during the '60s. It was their battle cry against war, against aggression, and against the perceived stereotypical attitudes that existed among their parents' generation.

The more young people began to experiment with drugs during the '60s, the more they *wanted* to experiment. It became a means to an end for them. Drugs gave them what they felt they needed in order to see beyond the unseen impregnable walls that existed within society. Drugs helped to break these walls down and gave them the courage to push for societal change.

Timothy Leary's phrase *"turn on, tune in, drop out"* became the expression of those who believed that finding peace meant first going deep *within* one's self, and this was accomplished easily via drugs like LSD. Leary first used the phrase in a speech in New York City in 1966. *"Like every great religion of the past we seek to **find the divinity within** and to express this revelation in a life of glorification and the worship of God. These ancient goals we define in the metaphor of the present — turn on, tune in, drop out."*[15]

I have emphasized the phrase "find the divinity within" because it encapsulates the agenda of some people during that time who were on the cutting edge of the 1960s playbook. In reality though, this desire to "find the divinity within" is no different from what the New Age movement had been teaching since the 1950s and before. In fact, it really goes back to Madame Blavatsky (1831-1891) and is then carried on by Alice Bailey (1880-1949), both of the Theosophist Society: Blavatsky in the United Kingdom and Bailey in the United States.

This is what many people do not realize about so many things that Satan has done *in* society. I've written about things before in several of my books[16] that prove how involved Satan has been in the development of society and the direction it has taken.

---

[15] "Transcript (for American Experience documentary on the Summer of Love)". PBS and WGBH. 2007-03-14.
[16] See *Demons in Disguise* and *Nephilim Nightmare* by the author, as two examples.

In reality, as I have pointed out in my books, Satan has provided something for everyone. If someone is really drawn to music, then Satan has a brand of music that literally strikes a chord within them while enriching them with words, phrases, and ideas that are literally born in hell. If someone has a penchant for philosophy, then there have been plenty of books and poets who have discussed the problem of the ages from the perspective of man's desire to learn to fly. That "flying" here is referencing our inner deity. In order to "fly" free of the chains that bind us, we first need to realize that we are *gods,* and then we need to learn to free that deity within us.

It can be safely stated that Satan has not left one stone unturned in his efforts to capture and enslave all people, regardless of their proclivities. Whatever someone's interests, Satan has found or even created a way to take advantage and draw a person deeper into his realm. I have to marvel that in the decade of the 1960s so much seemed to confront American society. It all happened so fast and was so tumultuous that we realize resistance seemed futile in many ways. Satan is a force to be reckoned with and what he attempts to accomplish is often accomplished, as God *allows.*

# Chapter 4
# Uninformed

W hat we have already discussed and highlighted are really only *symptoms* of the real problem that spent decades gurgling beneath the surface, only to force its way onto the scene during the 1960s.

However, the real problem is not what happened in the 1960s. It was not even due to the various things we have seen that took place during the transition period from the 1950s to the 1960s. The real problem actually goes back further in time to the 1930s, the time immediately *following* World War II. What we are dealing with *today* and what we've been dealing with for decades can be summed up in something that is referred to as *cultural Marxism* (or *political correctness*).

I truly wish I could explain in short order how cultural Marxism created the society that exists today, a society fraught with decay, loose morals, abject hatred of anything conservative, and immersed in the worship of anything on the Left. Unfortunately, it's going to take a good portion of this book to explain what it is we are talking about and how cultural Marxism (CM) and political correctness (PC) have not only taken *hold* but in many ways taken *over*.

I am going to try to keep things as simple as possible, though if we know anything about Marxism, we know that it is not a superficial subject but one of tremendous depth. At times it is difficult to explain it simply and often requires a good deal of verbiage. This is exactly why so many books have been written on the subject.

Let me start by speaking about how people in society have become "dumbed" down, yet they often see themselves as intelligent individuals. They see no glaring deficiencies between their worldview and how they relate to others in the world and actual truth or fact.

Let's begin with an event that took place in America several months ago that has forever changed the way people think about guns. Ever since the Sandy Hook shooting tragedy, people have over-reacted regarding situations that involve guns. I read recently that a seven-year-old student was suspended for carving his breakfast into a shape that somewhat resembled a gun.[17] The teacher who saw this young boy's artistic effort got "mad" at him. Look, we all know how dangerous strawberry tarts can be once they have been modeled to look like guns!

---

[17] http://www.foxnews.com/us/2013/03/02/boy-7-suspended-for-shaping-pastry-into-gun-dad-says/ (03/02/2013)

I have to wonder what was going on in that teacher's brain at the time. The kid has probably seen a thousand shows and movies in which guns are used and like most young boys sees them as part of our culture. But apparently you cannot talk about guns and you certainly cannot create one out of a strawberry tart! That is verboten!

Okay, so who is the low-information person in the above scenario? If the story was reported accurately, teacher who got "mad" at the young boy for carving what appeared to her to be a gun out of his strawberry tart is definitely a low-information educator.

But some good may come out of it. *"A Maryland state senator has crafted a bill to curb the zeal of public school officials who are tempted to suspend students as young as kindergarten for having things — or talking about things, or eating things — that represent guns, but aren't actually anything like real guns."*

*"The bill also includes a section mandating counseling for school officials who fail to distinguish between guns and things that resemble guns."*[18] With the way too many educators have hopped on the anti-gun bandwagon, it's almost as though they would not know critical thinking if it bit them, yet we are told that critical thinking skills are what educators teach children to have and use.

You know, when the apostle Paul told Timothy that there would be terrible times during the last days (cf. 2 Timothy 3:1ff), I did not realize he meant that as part of that situation people would become complete morons in the process! If you stop to think about it you can see that the deference shown to being politically correct has created people who cannot think their way out of a wet paper bag.

This rush to quell everything and anything that has to do with guns is absurd. There is absolutely no common sense related to it anymore. People simply want them banned. They want kids to stop drawing

---

[18] http://pjmedia.com/instapundit/164749/ (03/10/2013)

them and carving them out of things they eat. They want to pretend that all guns, all the time, are terribly bad, no exceptions.

However, just recently, Gov. Cuomo of New York stated that Hollywood crews filming in New York would not be held to the same standard as everyone else in New York due to the new hastily passed laws in that state. Hollywood producers and filmmakers would still be able to use real weapons (with blanks) on the set when filming in New York.

What is the matter with these people? Why is it okay to produce movie after movie, TV series after TV series where characters use guns at every turn, yet we are supposed to dismiss any type of negative impact on our culture? Again, why has common sense been tossed out? In this case, it has to do with the billions of dollars in revenue that New York State rakes in because of all the business that Hollywood does with that state.

It's always about the money, whether people want to admit it or not. Again, I'll say it. If the medical profession was able to "prove" that smoking and cigarette products in movies and TV (as well as video games) account for at least half of the young smokers, then why does this not translate to all the violence in those same venues, especially gun-related violence? Again, it makes no sense that we can prove smoking negatively impacts viewers but violence, sex, or the use of guns supposedly has no effect on those same viewers. Absurd.

So, we'll just leave Hollywood alone because after all, look at how much money they pour into communities. Look at all the jobs they create. Leave Hollywood alone. Don't even *think* to tell them that they should tone down the violence in the programming they create. How dare we do that because Hollywood is involved in creating art and artists need to be left alone to create. Except when those artists want to create something in which smoking or smoking products are featured. Then we need to tone that down because the medical profession has proved that it sends the wrong message to young viewers, with at least half of them deciding to take up the habit of smoking because of it.

No wonder our society is as it is today. Years ago, it was unheard of to see any form of nudity on TV. Swearing was exceedingly rare, but over time that has changed. About twenty to twenty-five years ago, swearing debuted, and now it is normal to hear on TV.

Shows like NYPD Blue also helped introduce viewers to nudity as well as swearing. For years, producers have argued that they can't compete with pay channels like HBO unless restrictions were loosened up. So what happened? Restrictions loosened up and the producers of shows like NYPD Blue got their way. It's supposed to reflect "real" television.

Before anyone misses my point, let me restate it. If we can prove that smoking negatively impacts people in society, then why does it not stand to reason that violence, nudity, and excessive gun violence can do the same? Do we really need to have studies on this in order to prove the connection?

I've read of women's groups complaining to Hollywood producers about the constant portrayal of women as weak and submissive or as simply sex objects. So what happened? Hollywood responded by creating women's characters who could kick butt! They can be as bad as their male counterparts. But I thought stereotypes have no negative impact on viewers? That's not what the medical profession or certain women's groups believe, and they have made enough noise to cause Hollywood to change the way they portray characters.

In fact, it is also clear that gay and lesbian groups believe that to constantly have TV shows, movies, games (or comic books) in which gay and lesbian characters are *absent* is not a good thing for gays and lesbians, or for society at large. Gays and lesbians want to be seen as normal, so how can they make that happen?  By ensuring that gay and lesbian characters are increasingly portrayed in TV shows, movies, video games, and comic books as average people.  Obviously, the reality is that viewers *are* affected by what we see in so many productions coming out of Hollywood, for good or bad.

These productions *do* fix or even change our thinking, don't they?  Please don't tell me that watching movies, TV shows, cartoons, video games, or reading comic books has no ability to affect the way people think and act.  I don't buy it and neither should you.  We are force-fed whatever Hollywood wants to ram down our throats.  The media – even news bureaus, such as they are – do the dirty work of creating images that we take to heart.  They present ways to think.  They do their level best to override how we think with how they want to portray things in society.

What is the point of advertising at all if the ads themselves have no effect on viewers?  Smart advertisers pay big bucks for what is known as product placement in sitcoms, episodic dramas, movies, video games, and the rest.  They know the score while the "experts" try to tell us the exact opposite.  Have you bought the lie?

Years ago, the good guy was the good guy.  He rarely used his gun, but when he did, it was to take down the *bad* guy.  Over the years the terms "good guy" and "bad guy" have, in some ways, become synonymous.  They are interchangeable, depending upon the situation.  We can have a good cop who goes rogue, but it's "okay" because he's still going after bad guys, though he becomes judge, jury, and executioner.

Society has become pitiful due to political correctness.  The complete loss of common sense is a real concern.  People fail to see it.  They fail to understand that they can't even make good decisions today because they are blinded by the inconsistencies created by their own *politically correct* thinking.  It's tragic.  Very tragic indeed.

Paul stated it perfectly. *"People will be lovers of themselves, lovers of money, boastful, proud, abusive, disobedient to their parents, ungrateful, unholy, without love, unforgiving, slanderous, without self-control, brutal, not lovers of the good, treacherous, rash, conceited, lovers of pleasure rather than lovers of God— having a form of godliness but denying its power"* (2 Timothy 3:1-6a).

If you stop to seriously consider it, you see that a lot of those character traits Paul mentions are created by a person's own tendency to be completely self-serving. However, some of those things are created due to an absolute loss of common sense and ability to think rationally. Again, this is due to an overexposure to politically correct thinking. It is so absurd, yet it persists throughout our society.

It is the same type of thinking that causes people to believe that banning guns will create a safer society, in spite of the fact that banning guns will only have any effect on law-abiding citizens, both coming and going. There is no common sense in play here. It is all based on emotional tyranny and most of it is from the people who fail to think rationally: the low-information persons.

Whether it's Maxine Waters stating that sequestration will destroy 170 million jobs (there are only 150 million jobs in the American workforce), Nancy Pelosi stating that we will lose 500 million jobs per month, some poor seven-year-old kid receiving a suspension notice for crafting what appears to be a gun to some low-information teacher, or something else entirely, the fact is that people are being dumbed down due to the cultural Marxism that has taken root in society, which translates to the way people think.

It is completely unnatural. God created people as intelligent beings, yet so much of what passes for "intelligence" these days is nothing more than stupidity as a result of politically correct thinking. This type of "thinking" makes little to no sense at all, yet it is treated as informed, intelligent, wise, and much more.

It's not. It's garbage and it only caters to the drivel spouted by those on the Left who are doing everything they can to resist God and His sovereignty. Their continued resistance is really futile.

There is absolutely nothing more tragic than watching an entire society turn into low-information people and do so by choice with open arms. I'm not a genius. There are tons of people smarter than me. Yet I can see what's happening, not just in America, but throughout the world.

What are we left with then? Again, we defer to the apostle Paul, who could not have said it better when he so eloquently stated in Romans 1:22 the following words: *"Professing to be wise, they became fools."*

That is probably the most tragic part of the whole thing. The teacher who got angry at the seven-year-old boy and anyone else who is held hostage by politically correct subterfuge actually believes that they are wise or intelligent people. Unfortunately, in the end they are anything but that.

I pray that God will open their eyes, if for no other reason than that they will realize their spiritual need for Him and His salvation. If He does not open their eyes, they will never be able to see the salvation message clearly, nor will they be able to receive it for themselves.

Certainly, God wants that for them. Are they willing to see the truth about themselves in order to receive the only salvation that can actually save them? Certainly, God wants that.

Let's pray that He makes it so.

# Chapter 5
# Cultural Marxism

St. Basil's Cathedral, Moscow

**P**olitical Correctness has been with us for some time. It is, by design, the umbrella under which society ensures that people – especially people of color – are not offended by people who are *not* people of color.

Political correctness has been one of the predominant tools that has helped create cultural Marxism throughout America. As I mentioned in my last chapter, cultural Marxism endeavors to produce a society that is free of traditional (specifically *biblical*) values, replacing those with something else entirely, something that is usually the polar opposite. It does so mainly by directing its assault against *reason*, encouraging the use of emotions to make decisions. Certainly, emotions can be used as *indicators*, though emotions alone should not be the sole decision-making faculty. But those who resort to and rely on emotion to make decisions often become slaves to *relativism*, which generates a type of emotional tyranny within that person, though they normally fail to see that.

Those who use political correctness do so in ways that appeal to the way a person feels about something. This is done purposefully because those wielding political correctness understand the true value of crafting an emotional pull in a person and how this sentiment can override the higher faculties like thought, reason, and logic itself.

*"When addressing the general public, contemporary advocates of Political Correctness – or Cultural Marxism, as it might just as easily be called – present their beliefs with appealing simplicity as merely a commitment to being 'sensitive' to other people and embracing values such as 'tolerance' and 'diversity.'*

*"The reality is different. Political Correctness is the use of culture as a sharp weapon to enforce new norms and to stigmatize those who dissent from the new dispensation; to stigmatize those who insist on values that will impede the new 'PC' regime: free speech and free and objective intellectual inquiry."*[19]

So what is essentially (at first) presented as simply being sensitive to others ultimately ends up being a way to force people to speak or act in a certain way. This ends up restricting the First Amendment without even passing a law.

But it is important to understand two things about cultural Marxism. First, *what is it?* and second, *where does it lead?* Another way to ask that is to ask *what is the purpose of creating cultural Marxism* in

---

[19] http://www.discoverthenetworks.org/viewSubCategory.asp?id=552 (03/03/2013)

America (or any nation or society for that matter)? What is the hoped-for conclusion? As we dig deeper into determining what comprises cultural Marxism, we will realize the answer to this question.

In order to better understand just exactly how America is being subdued, thwarted, and in the end, overtaken from within, we need to understand more about what cultural Marxism is and how it has made its inroads into the fabric of American society. Most I'm sure don't even recognize that what has been occurring within American society has a name at all.

We deferred to William S. Lind for his understanding of cultural Marxism in chapter one. Again, he notes that, *"Cultural Marxism is a branch of western Marxism, different from the Marxism-Leninism of the old Soviet Union. It is commonly known as 'multiculturalism' or, less formally, Political Correctness. From its beginning, the promoters of cultural Marxism have known they could be more effective if they concealed the Marxist nature of their work, hence the use of terms such as 'multiculturalism.'"*[20]

Lind also highlights the fact that while *economic Marxism* differs from that of *cultural Marxism*, the gap has been bridged by redefining Marxism so that it would fit the mold of American culture. In doing so, certain aspects of Marxism were (and remain) hidden from the public.

Those of us who taught in the public schools have long been aware of the term "multiculturalism." In essence, multiculturalism at its simplest point basically acknowledges that a culture is comprised of *numerous* cultures. That by itself tends to remove anything suspicious from it. Who cannot agree with that truth, because it *is* truth?

---

[20] http://www.marylandthursdaymeeting.com/Archives/SpecialWebDocuments/Cultural.Marxism.htm (03/04/2013)

Cultural diversity is also something that we often hear about when discussing various components of a particular culture. The problem with multiculturalism is that it too often focuses on specific aspects of one particular culture within the larger culture. In such a situation, for instance, Islam is seen as deserving respect because of its differences (as well as its third world origins), and as such should be allowed to flourish when those of Islam become part of another *existing* culture and in spite of the fact that many within Islam show no signs of wanting to adopt aspects of the new culture of which they have become part.

Multiculturalism allows for and even encourages these differences. However, as we have seen throughout the world, the onus is not on Islam to assimilate, but the pressure is on America (or another culture) to allow for Islamic *excesses*, in spite of the fact that these excesses fly in the face of the new culture in which Islamists have now taken up residence. This is encouraged in the name of diversity or co-existence.

This is, I believe, what Obama was getting at when he stated that *"The future must not belong to those who slander the prophet of Islam."*[21] Mr. Obama essentially wound up elevating Islam above other cultures with that one statement and insisted that people should be very wary of doing or saying things that might offend Muslims.

He followed that statement up with *"But to be credible, those who condemn that slander must also condemn the hate we see and the images of Jesus Christ that are desecrated or churches that are destroyed. Or the Holocaust that is denied."*[22] Unfortunately, Obama's first comment singling out Islam has greater weight in this context than his follow-up comments about Jesus and the Holocaust.

---

[21] http://www.mediaite.com/tv/obamas-tragic-pander-the-future-must-not-belong-to-those-who-slander-the-prophet-of-islam/ (03/04/2013)
[22] Ibid

Multiculturalism succeeds where *"immigrant societies, while preserving their cultural habits and religious beliefs in the private sphere, make every effort to integrate into the public domain, to respect the laws, assumptions and folkways of their host, and to contribute to the economic vitality of their adopted country..."*[23] Clearly, this speaks of immigrants who come to America and who do their level best to become part of the fabric of America by learning the language, learning and obeying the laws of this land, and instead of relying on welfare, become active, productive members of society who work and pay taxes. This is when multiculturalism works. In this scenario, the immigrant is not expected to discard the culture to which they were born. They are simply expected to – in addition to continuing to practice aspects of their native culture – take on the values and norms of their newly adopted culture.

The problem, of course, is that this rarely seems to happen, and there is little in place (in America) to encourage it. More often than not, multiculturalism seeks to publicly *expose* the differences between the races and ethnicities rather than focusing on the commonalities. This is why, in 2013, we still have Affirmative Action, along with specific groups that cater to gender and race issues. It is *politically correct* to have them (though many believe them to be a form of racism in and of themselves) and those who complain against them are labeled racists, bigots, sexists, or all three.

This is also why notes and flyers sent home to parents of schoolchildren are often written in many different languages so that parents can read them. Unfortunately, as we have learned, many people who come to America from various cultures only know how to *speak* their native tongue and are often unable to read or write it. Creating flyers that are translated into many languages is often a complete waste of

---

[23] http://www.mediaite.com/tv/obamas-tragic-pander-the-future-must-not-belong-to-those-who-slander-the-prophet-of-islam/ (03/04/2013)

the taxpayer dollar, especially given the fact that rarely do other countries practice this same type of thing.

In truth, the multiculturalism that has flourished in America has too often been seriously divisive, literally pitting one race or ethnicity against another. Rather than people wanting to become *part* of that new culture (while continuing to appreciate their own), they insist on retaining their own cultural diversity in *public* without adopting aspects of their new culture. They wind up thumbing their noses at the culture of the country which they say is their newly adopted country. In essence, they simply *live* in that new country. They have adopted nothing, though they learn how to take advantage of the system so as to benefit themselves as they see fit.

Years ago, with the official founding of America, most people came through Ellis Island to gain legal entrance into this country. Yes, they looked for neighborhoods in which they would hear their own language, smell the food they were familiar with, and share their common culture with others like themselves. However, this does not mean they refused to learn English or abide by the laws of their newly adopted country, America. In essence, while they kept the values of the culture from which they were born, they readily adopted the culture of America.

This has not been the case for decades and generations. Slowly, consistently, people who have come to this country have insisted on remaining aloof. They show their disdain for America in spite of the fact that their life here is far superior to what it was in the country from which they came. Does the phrase "familiarity breeds contempt" come into play here? I think so.

That disdain is actually encouraged by various groups in America and the fact that their own ethnicity is valued over and above their union with America is greater cause for concern. In short, multiculturalism has played havoc with societies where it has been tried. Unfortunately, it has become tremendously ensconced in cultures like America (or Great Britain, or France) and pushing back against it is difficult at best.

In America, CAIR (Council on American-Islamic Relations) exists to ensure that Muslims are allowed to practice their religion and live their lives as freely as possible. The Islamic ideology is allowed to flourish, and because of CAIR (and other groups in the United States) there has been a great push to use Sharia law (Islamic law) within United States' courts instead of the Constitution and Bill of Rights. This is really treasonous, yet there are politicians who support this.

Multiculturalism, which is simply an aspect of cultural Marxism (or political correctness), came to America's shores decades ago. It did not start in the 1950s, nor did it start in the 1960s. It actually started in earnest just after World War I, just prior to the 1920s. That may not seem to be the case, but it can easily be traced back to that time period.

What we saw during the time going from the 1950s to the 1960s was that multiculturalism, cultural Marxism, and political correctness came out of the closet, so to speak. From the 1960s onward it became much more obvious, yet it was not really connected to any recognized form of Marxism since that term was never used publicly. Instead, the safe-sounding "multiculturalism" and "political correctness" were adopted. Who could argue that we should not be sensitive to what we said and thought so as to avoid offending people who fell into groups that were labeled "victims"?

Yet, consider if someone who was not familiar with the way your family worked and played came to your own home. Would *you* be expected to walk on eggshells around them? Would *you* be expected to not have certain foods, or not pray before meals, or not speak in certain ways so as not to offend, in your own home? Wouldn't the onus be on the people *visiting* your home? They are in *your* home and while we always want to treat guests well, the reality is that it would be completely unfair of your guest(s) to expect you to change your routine just for him, wouldn't it?

Regrettably, for some time this has been the case in many countries including America and is seen most clearly with respect to the immigration of millions of Muslims. Dearborn, MI is now often referred to as "Dearbornistan" by many because not only is there a very large contingent of Muslims there, but they have endeavored to take over, inserting a mentality into the culture that looks to Sharia law as the means and way of Islam. They have power in numbers and they know it. Far from wanting to become part of America, they wish to overthrow it. Certainly, not all Muslims think like this, but it is clear that too many do. They are not so much interested in obtaining a piece of the pie but in reality want to turn the part of America in which they now dwell into an Islamic community, guided by Islamic principles and law.

In essence, cultural Marxism is *"a movement that seeks the elimination of codes of behavior, binding obligations, and moral standards."*[24] This statement appears at odds with what I have just described regarding Islam. However, cultural Marxism is used to turn things upside down so that what was traditional will ultimately be replaced by something else entirely. Islam *also* seeks to overthrow the traditions of a culture it moves into and it does so by sheer numbers and even force if necessary. In case you haven't been paying attention, there are many within Islam that believe Islam *will* yet rule the world in complete autonomy. It is to this end they work.

While on one hand, cultural Marxism assumes that everyone is equal (a seemingly noble cause), it attempts to create that equality by first setting up arbitrary boundaries between races, ethnicities, and gen-

---

[24] http://www.americanthinker.com/2012/11/the_new_normal_turning_back_cultural_marxism.html#ixzz2Mb2oYArq (03/04/2013)

ders that wind up highlighting the *majority* race or ethnicity. Then, once the majority race or ethnicity has been subdued or negated through the use of political correctness, the minority races or ethnicities become the majority. Yet the practice of political correctness continues.

Because of this, it stands to reason that certain aspects of America's founding moral code would be attacked: namely, the biblical standards. In too many cases, our founding fathers – because they were of the majority (white aristocracy) – are seen as evil and oppressors of the poor. This same argument is used today.

For cultural Marxism to succeed, those who agree with the standards set by the founders of this nation also need to be overthrown. This is why conservatives who are also people of color are often vilified by those on the Left: because those conservatives side with the founding fathers that promulgated the values that are part of our founding documents.

Many believe that the implementation of modern-day cultural Marxism has roots in the thinking and philosophy of Jean-Jacques Rousseau (1712-1778). Just as today's Cultural Marxist often reacts to culture from the belly of *emotion*, so did Rousseau. "*In his Discourse on the Origin of Inequality, Rousseau started his attack at the foundation of the Enlightenment project: Reason.*"[25]

To Rousseau, the "*root of [civilization's] moral degradation is* **reason**, *the original sin of humankind.*"[26] This is actually the exact opposite of what the Bible teaches. It is not reason per se that gave way to original sin, but the *emotional influence* of *faulty* reasoning.

---

[25] http://www.stephenhicks.org/2010/01/05/rousseaus-counter-enlightenment/ (03/40/2013)
[26] http://www.stephenhicks.org/2010/01/05/rousseaus-counter-enlightenment/ (03/40/2013; emphasis added)

Adam and Eve were tempted to eat of the tree of forbidden fruit in spite of the fact that they had been specifically told by God Himself that to do so would mean certain *death*. This came to pass as they first died *spiritually* and also began to die *physically*. It was their *emotional* response to the tree's fruit and their willingness to consider the deceptive words of the Tempter that caused them to disobey God by eating the fruit, not *reason*.

In reality, their sin *began* in their hearts: their *emotion*. They *wanted* to eat of the fruit, so their will caused them to do it. The lust for freedom *began* with their *emotional desire*. The actual act of eating the fruit simply proved that sin begins within the heart of a person, just as Jesus said it does in His Sermon on the Mount of Matthew 5.

Had Adam and Eve persisted in obedience to God's truthful reasoning – *eat and die* – they would have remained sinless and would not have experienced death. It was their *emotion* that prompted them to give ear to new "reasoning," reasoning which brought about their ultimate demise and corrupted all of God's Creation.

So Rousseau attacked the period known as the Enlightenment by claiming that reason is the death knell for civilization. Reasoning that leads to absolute *truth* is always the best way since our feelings and emotions can bring about a false perception of something, even when that something is absolute truth.

In American society, we recognize that our founding fathers created a country that was based on biblical principles. These principles are tested, known, and understood to be full of veracity. Reason cannot cause people to disown them. However, *faulty* reasoning – reasoning based not on truth, but on *emotion* – can create a desire to overthrow those biblical principles.

To Rousseau (and others who believe as he did), *reason* is the problem, not the solution. Reason has created the mess civilization is in.

Reason caused all sorts of problems in society, not least of which is the "haves" and the "have nots." Reason would cause some individuals to create ways of making themselves very rich at the expense of the rest of society. Because people could *reason*, it was not long before inventions occurred as well as ways to live better lives. To Rousseau, this created problems because as he believed, reason creates *selfish awareness*: a desire to serve self.

*"The reason that made civilization's inequalities possible also made the better-off uncaring about the suffering of the less fortunate. Reason, according to Rousseau, is opposed to compassion: Reason generates civilization, which is the ultimate cause of the sufferings of the victims of inequality, but reason also then creates rationales for ignoring that suffering."*[27]

So in Rousseau's opinion, serving self (or what he called *egocentrism*) created the ills of society and he believes this occurred with the onset of *reason*. Without reason, there would be none of these ills, according to Rousseau. *"Reason is what engenders egocentrism...and reflection strengthens it. Reason is what turns man in upon himself. Reason is what separates him from all that troubles him and afflicts him. Philosophy is what isolates him and what moves him to say in secret, at the sight of a suffering man, 'Perish if you will; I am safe and sound.'"*[28]

I would contend – as does the Bible – that man turns in upon himself due to the fallen nature, which has nothing to do with accurate or truthful reasoning at all but a morbid feeling that we need to be constantly placating self. Again, this is what was really behind the fall of Adam and Eve. It stemmed from the inordinate desire to cater to self in spite of the truth (reason) that God had explained to them about what would occur if they chose to ignore His warnings.

---

[27] http://www.stephenhicks.org/2010/01/05/rousseaus-counter-enlightenment/ (03/40/2013)
[28] Ibid

It was not reason that drew Adam or Eve to the fruit in the first place. It was emotion. Had neither Eve nor Adam been *emotionally* drawn to the tree's fruit, or emotionally drawn to be *separate* from God's mandates, the Tempter would not have been able to make a strong enough case to get them to sin. But the temptation became something that triggered their emotions and it was that emotional pull that was created that brought about their failure to resist temptation and obey through reason. *Reason* was not the problem. *Emotion* was the problem.

We see this throughout society today. People too often react from their emotions, not from reason, and certainly not from right thinking. I dealt with this previously in the chapter titled *Uninformed*. This type of person knows little of reason based on factual information (or absolute truth). They only know how to respond to life's situations through *emotion*. They want something, so that is what they go after, irrespective of what reason might tell them of whether or not it is an appropriate pursuit.

Reason is going the way of the dinosaur. It is being dismissed from society and from civilization in general by a growing number of people every day. Reason doesn't really exist anymore. Instead, emotion (based on faulty thinking) rules the mind of too many people.

People wanted Obama to win re-election so they voted for him multiple times, as we are finding out and as they have admitted in spite of the fact that this is illegal. People want to receive free money or free phones from our government in spite of reason that says it cannot last forever, and that is what they pursue until they have what their emotion says they want. It is the emotional pull that creates their direction in life, not reason.

Reason does not guide many in society anymore. Emotional blindness does, and because of it society has become *feeling-oriented* and *dumbed down*. People are no longer *able* to reason through situations using the solid base of biblical virtue.  They see no value in it.  They only see value in what they want from society, whether they deserve it or not.  Though this is completely *unreasonable*, these people never stop to consider that they are wrong in their thinking.  Do they have the capacity to even understand this?  It is doubtful.

God did not make human beings to live our lives based on feelings.  Yes, He gave us emotions, but emotions should not guide us.  It is fine when our emotions react appropriately to situations as indicators.  When someone we love dies, we cry.  When we hear something funny, we laugh.  These are proper expressions of our emotions.  Yet for too many people, emotions guide the way they live their lives.  If they are so angry with someone that they would like to harm that person, they *do* harm them and justify their actions with an attempt at reason, but the reasons they use have nothing to do with logic or truth.  Their reasoning is still based on the way they *feel* about someone or something.

Much of cultural Marxism today has been stimulated by people like Rousseau.  It's the way they think and their thinking has permeated society and civilization.  They have endeavored to help people become *worse* than animals, which at least live by *instinct*.  Animals do not live by emotion.  Emotion is part of their life, but they don't live by it.  Wild animals hunt to survive.  They understand (through a form of instinctual reasoning) that without food, they will die.  Therefore, they hunt.

Animals don't necessarily kill because they *enjoy* killing (though because of the fall of humanity and the curse on Creation, it is likely that some animals do stupid things because of it). They kill because they need to eat or because that other animal is somehow seen as a threat to their own survival.

In chasing after emotional "needs" people have become enslaved to these emotions and react from that vantage point.  They do not react based on their reasoning at all. If they argue that they are using reasoning, it is faulty at best, not truthfully (or biblically) sound.

If you look at the way the Left routinely thinks, it becomes clear that they do not approach the Bible as absolute truth. That is obvious. If they reference the Bible at all, to them it is *relative* truth. The Bible is seen as a movable palette of truth, to be used where it can be made to fit into certain situations. It is not absolute truth by any stretch for those on the Left, if they even acknowledge the Bible at all.

This is not the way the authentic Christian sees the Bible. To the true conservative Christian, the Bible is absolute in its unerring presentation of truth that is applicable to all situations, regardless of the way people may *feel* about the Bible and what it has to say. There are plenty of people on the Left who *claim* to be Christian. Some even have "Rev" in front of their name. Unfortunately, their understanding of the Bible belies the fact that they do not view it as the final authority on anything. It is merely a set of instructions or guidelines that allows the goal post to be moved as a person (or group) sees fit.

The Bible is either absolute truth or it represents no truth at all. It says one thing or nothing. This is the biggest reason why those who insist on and pursue cultural Marxism seek to move American society *away* from biblical principles, because they are very aware of the fact that as long as people revere the Bible, accepting it as authoritative, no real ultimate progress toward a society fully based on cultural Marxism can exist or last.

> *"Rousseau-inspired cultural Marxists aim to convert [the United States] from a virtue-based community to a wilderness of wildly autonomous selves. In Rousseau's own words, these elites seek to 'force us to be free' -- free in particular from self-evident and objective truth."*[29]

---

[29] http://www.americanthinker.com/2012/11/the_new_normal_turning_back_cultural_marxism.html#ixzz2Mb2oYArq (03/04/2013)

Cultural Marxism cannot work if society is based solidly on the Bible or even the US Constitution or Bill of Rights. These documents and texts are resolute, guaranteeing certain rights and responsibilities. They invoke the blessings of God and seek to cause us to look *beyond* ourselves and to Him for His purposes. Moreover, those who take public office and who swear on the Bible during their oath promise to protect and defend the US Constitution. For too many politicians, though, this is a debatable point.

Rousseau wanted biblical *morality* to be replaced with *amorality*. This can only be accomplished when society moves away from, in this case, America's original moorings to biblical principles. It cannot happen as long as the Bible and biblical principles from it course through American society. Biblical morality must be overthrown.

This is why Islam, for instance, is given such freedom to do what Muslims believe needs to be done in America. Instead of inspiring them to assimilate into American culture they are encouraged to remain as they are and attempt to force *American* culture to capitulate. It is what gives rise to the attitude recently heard in Executive Director of CAIR Mustafa Carroll's words, "*If we are practicing Muslims, we are above the law of the land,*"[30] which were recently spoken at an outdoor event in Texas. This is too often the mindset of Muslims. They need obey no one but Allah. With this type of attitude, it is easy to see that we are all on the road to confrontation and it won't end well.

Rather than embracing aspects of American society, officials of CAIR are frequently at odds with the laws of this nation (and others). As such, they constantly take up one lawsuit after another over aspects of American society with which they disagree. They hope to change

---

[30] http://frontpagemag.com/2013/dgreenfield/dallas-cair-director-muslims-are-above-the-law-of-the-land/comment-page-1/#comment-4335821 (03/04/2013)

society to reflect their beliefs, which are based on the Qur'an and Sharia law.

Why do many Muslims disagree? Because, as Carroll stated, "*Islam does not have Texas in the current condition, the current socio-political condition that Texas is in. What is this condition that Texas is in? Why is Texas on the brink, when you look at Texas in comparison to 50 states, education, percent of population graduating from high school is 46, high school completion rate is 46, the scholastic assessment rate, the SAT score in Texas is 47, the percentage of population with no health insurance in Texas is first, those without health insurance Texas is first. When you look at the state of a child in Texas, the percentage of uninsured children, Texas is first...You shouldn't be filing legislation against Islam, when you look at Texas, Islam is not the problem. Islam is the solution. Allah Akbar.*"[31] This is stated and believed by many because Islam is seen as the "victim" among the politically correct.

This is the new morality that is at severe odds with biblical morality, on which the United States law and founding documents are based. In truth, this new morality is really *amorality* and it is solidly anti-biblical. It can do nothing to create a better society just as it can do nothing to create a better human being. That does not matter to Cultural Marxists because ultimately what they want is the pursuit of freedom solely for freedom's sake. This will happen – they believe – with the removal of biblical standards. In the end, what they wind up with is something far less than true freedom.

"*A move away from love-based virtue toward self-based autonomy is unreasonable and a flight from truth. Contrary to the opinion of many who pursue freedom merely for freedom's sake, modern radical autonomy has victims, as did its Jacobin predecessor. And, finally, cultural Marxism will result in a slothful societal euthanasia. The real question*

---

[31] http://frontpagemag.com/2013/dgreenfield/dallas-cair-director-muslims-are-above-the-law-of-the-land/comment-page-1/#comment-4335821 (03/04/2013)

*is whether the country will reject cultural Marxism as a near-term act of will or a by-default act of extinction."*[32]

---

[32] http://www.americanthinker.com/2012/11/the_new_normal_turning_back_cultural_marxism.html#ixzz2Mb2oYArq (03/04/2013)

# Chapter 6
# Racial Injustice

I couldn't believe it when I read it. I *still* can't believe, but there it was in black and white. It was in a report from the Inspector General regarding the inside of one division within the Department of Justice (DOJ) and the racialist dysfunction there. I first came across this at J. Christian Adams's website.[33]

---

[33] http://pjmedia.com/jchristianadams/2013/03/12/breaking-inspector-general-report-on-racialist-disfunction-inside-doj/ (03/22/2013)

This has – interestingly enough – come to light at the same time that Tom Perez's name has been bandied about as the man Obama wants as Labor Secretary. What's the connection? Perez is the Assistant Attorney General for the Civil Rights Division of the United States Department of Justice.

If you're interested in reading the entire 250-page report from the Inspector General, if you are viewing this book online you can click on the bottom of this page to download the PDF document for yourself.[34] If you are reading the print book, type the link at the bottom of the page into your internet browser and you will be able to read or print the PDF document.

You'll note that the report has to do specifically with the Voting Section of Civil Rights. In referencing the report, Adams points out that it *"was prepared in response to Representative Frank Wolf's (R-VA) outrage over the New Black* Panther *voter intimidation dismissal. In response to the report, Rep. Wolf said today, the 'report makes clear that the division has become a rat's nest of unacceptable and unprofessional actions, and even outright threats against career attorneys and systemic mismanagement.'*

*"Former Voting Section Chief Chris Coates and I both testified about the hostility towards race-neutral law enforcement by the Justice Department."*[35]

The New Black Panther voter intimidation situation is referring to the time in 2008 when several New Black Panther members in Philadelphia were video-taped standing outside one particular voting precinct, near the door to the precinct. One of the members carried what appeared to be a nightstick.

---

[34] http://www.justice.gov/oig/reports/2013/s1303.pdf (03/22/2013)
[35] http://pjmedia.com/jchristianadams/2013/03/12/breaking-inspector-general-report-on-racialist-disfunction-inside-doj/ (03/22/2013)

The two were eventually arrested, charged, and found guilty, but during the time they were found guilty and awaiting sentencing, the DOJ (of which Eric Holder had just taken the reins of leadership) essentially made the case evaporate completely. It was as if the situation never occurred.

In another case known as the Noxubee (Mississippi) case it was alleged that whites became victims of voter intimidation. Why did the DOJ refuse to step in and do anything about it? According to the report, it was "*because White citizens were not historical victims of discrimination or could fend for themselves.*"[36] So apparently, because there is no history of victimization and because we all allegedly have enough money to fight our own battles, we don't need to rely on the DOJ. In reality, the DOJ is there to protect *every* citizen of America, regardless of race, creed, or religion.

There you have it. So, because white people are not considered "*historical victims of discrimination*" white people have no claims through the system. In essence then the DOJ – Eric Holder's DOJ (of which Tom Perez is part and is currently being readied to take over as Labor Secretary) – obviously has no interest at all in helping white people who are victimized by blacks. Whites are on their own.

Now we actually have a report that details a plethora of racist policies within the Voting Section of the Civil Rights Division of the DOJ led by Tom Perez, Obama's pick to be Labor Secretary of the US This is amazing, but don't expect to see this on CNN. May not even make FOX News.

Yet what did the Left do when these allegations hit the fan several years ago? The very same thing they do today. They cry. They whine. They name-call and they do everything in their power to denounce, castigate, and denigrate those who would deign to believe

---

[36] http://pjmedia.com/jchristianadams/2013/03/12/breaking-inspector-general-report-on-racialist-disfunction-inside-doj/ (03/22/2013)

that there could possibly be members of the black community who are racist toward whites. Apparently, racism is something only whites can actually be responsible for because we have no victimization history.

One Lefty from 2010 put it this way: *"Race-baiting has been a central element to the phony New Black Panthers scandal from the start, despite the fact that right-wing activist J. Christian Adams' accusations do not stand up to the evidence. But court filings earlier this week, in which the Obama Justice Department is asking a federal court to extend its injunction against black leaders in Mississippi for discriminating against white voters, should end once and for all the scurrilous accusation that the Obama administration is hostile to prosecuting black defendants on behalf of white victims."*[37]

Those words were written by Jeremy Holden, Director of Research at Media Matters. For those who are not aware, Media Matters is funded by George Soros.

But let's look at Holden's verbal assault. He comes out of the chute with a charge of race-baiting and adds to that charge the label "right-wing activist" against J. Christian Adams. But here we are about three years later and the case is not only *still* here, but apparently there is a report from the Inspector General outlining severe problems in which racial division *was* fomented by Tom Perez's division within the DOJ. Well, how do you like that? You mean *"right-wing activist"* and *"race-baiter"* J. Christian Adams was right all along? Apparently, and this simply tells us that despite facts, political correctness often makes inroads into society.

This is what the Left does. They come out with both barrels firing off rounds, hoping that if they attack quickly enough and with enough fervor people will believe that they (the Leftists) are correct. It

---

[37] http://mediamatters.org/blog/2010/07/16/adams-case-falls-apart-even-further/167813 (03/22/2013)

works often because these people are not stupid. They are in fact very well-informed, informed enough to know how to twist the truth to make it appear as lies while they take their lies and replace the truth with them.

In the quote above, Holden very confidently states that the accusations from Adams *"do not stand up to the evidence,"* and he even bolded that text in his original article. That alone is designed to convince people that he is correct because how could he even make such a statement if it was not true? Leftists do it all the time. They do it with a straight face too. They could fool a lie detector.

But again, here we are nearly three years later and the Inspector General has uncovered a great deal more than Holden would ever admit to. In fact, he'll likely pooh-pooh it, completely downplaying it as if the facts of the case are so transparently false it doesn't even require the time it takes for him to offer a rebuttal. That's another thing Leftists do. They redirect.

What's interesting about the Noxubee (Mississippi) case – as we learn from the report – is that whites weren't the only ones who were victimized. Apparently, parties within the DOJ even threatened blacks who wanted to do the right thing! They were silenced. Moreover, Voting Section Chief Chris Coates was allegedly becoming a big problem because he was actually pursuing justice when he was shut down by Holder at the request of Acting Assistant Attorney General Loretta King, who complained about Coates. Apparently, *"King didn't like that Coates was willing to use civil rights laws to protect white voters."*[38] Is it possible that civil rights laws are only for minorities and probably mainly for blacks at that?

Oh, but Jeremy Holden and all his Left-wing buds at Soros-funded Media Matters told us in no uncertain terms back in 2010 that there

---

[38] http://pjmedia.com/jchristianadams/2013/03/12/breaking-inspector-general-report-on-racialist-disfunction-inside-doj/ (03/22/2013)

was nothing to see here!  Those nasty right-wingers were barking up an empty tree...again!

Here's the deal, folks.  Cultural Marxism has gained a very solid footing in the United States and it's largely because of people like George Soros who have an interest in bringing America to a complete collapse and have the finances to do it.

These people peddle lies.  That's what they do.  They come across as confident, even caring, but everything about them is a bold-faced lie.  If there was absolutely no profit in what they were doing, they wouldn't be doing it.  They obviously will gain tremendously if they succeed.  They need to keep people enslaved to the false ideas that are spewed from the Left.  They need to have and maintain control over them.

This is *why* they do *what* they do.  It's the need for control and they are working harder than ever to gain and keep that control.  But it may be that cracks are starting to appear and we can take advantage of those cracks.

# Chapter 7
# Subjective Virtue

One of the books I have been reading is by Anthony Browne and is called *The Retreat of Reason* (2006). The subtitle is "*Political correctness and the corruption of public debate in modern Britain.*" It is amazing to me how there are so many out there who seem to understand the problem, yet there are more who are happy to deny it. All following quotes are taken from his book.

As I have said before, cultural Marxism (as opposed to economic Marxism) is something that has been advancing throughout American society. However, it first took root in British society.

Browne states, "*Political correctness started as a study of cultural Marxism in Germany in the 1920s, and was adopted by the 1960s counter culture, eager to promote tolerance and alternatives to the conservative values of the time.*"

Browne notes though how quickly political correctness became part of and took over academia in the US. After going full circle throughout the West, he states that in 1997, "*Britain became governed for the first time by a government largely controlled by politically-correct ideology.*"

The interesting thing about political correctness is that no matter how it started – what the intentions were then – it was essentially a reaction to the "*dominant ideology*" of the time, eventually replacing that originally dominant ideology with itself. I would fully agree with him that political correctness "*has replaced reason with emotion, subordinating objective truth to subjective virtue.*"

Anthony Browne also notes one other extremely important factor about political correctness prior to defining it. He says that "*the aim of political correctness is to redistribute power from the powerful to the powerless. It automatically and unquestioningly supports those it deems victims, irrespective of whether they merit it, and opposes the powerful, irrespective of whether they are malign or benign. For the politically correct, the West, the US and the multinational corporations can do no good, and the developing world can do no wrong.*" Hence, we see the Marxist implications of political correctness. Of course, it makes sense why people like Michael Moore would never want to be seen as capitalists! They must continue the illusion (lie) that they are not part of the 1% and in reality are just like everyone else who is struggling to survive, in spite of the fact that Moore is not at all struggling to survive.

We have seen the awfulness and unfairness of political correctness gone awry in places like the Netherlands where Islam was almost completely able to take over the political landscape of that country. The same type of thing regarding the HIV virus occurred in Britain, where as Browne explains, the influx of African immigrants brought in high incidents of HIV, yet no one wanted to discuss it because it appeared to be racist. The facts were ignored for two years in favor of issuing "safe sex" campaigns for heterosexuals, but the real problem was not with heterosexuals having unprotected sex with either heterosexuals or bisexuals and then contracting HIV. The real problem that could not be discussed (due to political correctness) had to do with the fact that the virus was being brought into Britain through immigrants from Africa.

While Browne believes that political correctness did have a good purpose when it began, it has now definitely grown past those purposes and is doing far greater harm to society than any good.

It is similar to unions. When unions first began, they were desperately needed because there was virtually no protection for the worker in America. They were being abused with long, hard hours, unsafe working conditions, and essentially no breaks at all. They worked twelve to fourteen hour days, without overtime.

So workers rallied together and fought the system. Eventually, though it was often a tremendous uphill battle, unions were formed to protect the workers from the unsafe, unfair, and careless demands of the management. Things began to improve for the workers almost immediately. Wages became better, hours were normalized, and eventually, even healthcare became part of the process.

But today, unions have become what management was prior to those unions originally forming. Now unions are powerful and often more powerful than management. Their demands are often unattainable by management. Because they have no place to go but up, unions continue to make unrealistic demands on companies and management that in some cases (like Hostess) shut down companies altogether. This is as opposed to working with management to come to agreements that benefit both worker and management. Unions continue to see management as the evil entity that needs to be overcome, in spite of the fact that too often management cannot continue to bend to the will of unions without doing tremendous harm to the company that employs the workers.

This is the way political correctness has evolved. What began as something that could benefit society has become a dragon that is beyond control yet controls nearly every part of society. As we look back over the pages of history, we see where reason has taken a backseat to emotion. Rather than being able to discuss things responsibly, reasonably, and without negative emotion, political correctness dictates that certain subjects are forbidden and anyone who cannot agree with those who use political correctness to form his views needs to be shut down and seen as the villain.

It is not unusual to be called a "hater" when it comes to sharing an opinion about homosexuality that goes against the established politically correct norm. If someone says, "I believe the Bible teaches that homosexuality is wrong," he is verbally attacked by the politically correct crowd instantly and labeled a "hater" in spite of the fact that there might be absolutely no indication that hatred undergirded his utterance about homosexuality or was part of his thinking.

In instances like this, Browne points out that *"The Politically Correct are more intolerant of dissent than traditional liberals or even conservatives. Liberals of earlier generations accepted unorthodoxy as normal. Indeed the right to differ was a datum of classical liberalism. The Politically Correct do not give that right a high priority. It distresses their programmed minds.* ***Those who do not conform should be ignored, silenced or vilified****. There is a kind of soft totalitarianism about Political Correctness."* [emphasis added]

This is exactly why people like Ed Schultz, Chris Matthews, Lawrence O'Donnell, and way too many to count seem to fly off the handle at a second's notice. They cannot emotionally handle the fact that people are saying something that to them is politically incorrect. It doesn't matter whether it's true or not. This flies in the face of the way they feel about something. They believe their political correctness gives them the right to castigate, denigrate, vilify, blame, and silence those who are not politically correct. It is because they are not politically correct that they "deserve" the response they receive, and that is not only allowed but encouraged under the unwritten terms of political correctness.

In essence then, political correctness, in attempting to do something that was good, has created a situation in society where it is perfectly fine to shut someone with whom a person does not agree down if that person is outside of the politically correct arena. This is what has dumbed down and inflamed segments of society. It has removed civility and shut down true discussion.

The true liberal then has normally been one who would allow dissent and discussion without remonstrating (this is key). Their demeanor was essentially one in which though they might disagree with a person, they would fight to the death for their right to have and express that opinion. Today? A person who has a dissenting opinion (one that is not understood as being politically correct) is verbally attacked. This is what political correctness has done to society.

If we went back through the New Testament we would find that just as Jesus was not what we would consider to be politically correct then and was ultimately crucified because of it, He will evidence the same type of anti-political correctness when He returns. He would actually deign to point out the sins of people that He met today if He was physically here wandering the streets of cities. He would tell people what they should avoid doing and to "*go and sin no more.*" It is not politically correct to talk of sin today, or hell, or to discuss homosexuality in what someone might consider to be a negative light.

Political correctness tosses out the ability to simply discuss and even disagree over issues. Instead, the arena of debate has become a war zone. How many times have we seen this on television or heard it on the radio? Someone will have some guest on their show with an opposing opinion and it is not long before a person begins to attack the other solely for having an opposing opinion. The goal is to shut them down: to silence them.

How often have we listened while guest and host talk over each other and do their level best to drown the other person out? Even on those shows where no guest is included, the host has a field day calling people names or labeling them as racist or sexist, and they do it with a vehemence that would curdle milk.

This is what political correctness has created for society. We see this so easily with Mr. Obama, as just one example. As a person of color, the politically correct individual cannot wait to label a person who disagrees with Obama's policies as racist. It doesn't matter that many of his policies were the same ones Clinton tried to enact; Clinton was *white* so those who disagreed with him (and were white) could not be accurately called racists then. Now, we can be. It is done to shut down conversation and that is exactly what political correctness does. It censors the "aggressor" so that the perceived "victim" is given "freedom" and "equality."

It is what has become of society these days because political correctness as a form of cultural Marxism is working its way through society to topple what was, replacing it with an unwritten code of acceptable speech, or what are commonly known as "speech codes."

Browne defers to William Lind, who has his own views about political correctness. "*The cultural Marxism of Political Correctness, like economic Marxism, has a single factor explanation of history. Economic Marxism says that all of history is determined by ownership of means of production. Cultural Marxism, or Political Correctness, says that all history is determined by power, by which groups defined in terms of race, sex, etc., have power over which other groups. Nothing else matters."*

Browne also quotes Richard Bernstein (NY Times Culture Correspondent) from his book *The Dictatorship of Virtue.* In 1990, he stated, "*Central to pc-ness, which has its roots in 1960s radicalism, is the view that Western society has for centuries been dominated by what is often called 'the white male power structure' or 'Patriarchal hegemony.' A related belief is that everybody but white heterosexual males has suffered some form of repression and been denied a cultural voice.*"

Browne goes on to point out that it used to be that those who favored liberalism's values (opposing traditional hierarchies, insulting men, promoting homosexuality, or doing what they could to redistribute power), including the freedom to attack western culture and values, were free to do so. Those who disagreed were free to challenge those notions that favored conservatism. That has changed because over time political correctness has worked to silence the dissenting viewpoint that is seen as punishing "victims."

Browne eventually comes round to defining political correctness on his terms. He says that it is "*an ideology that classifies certain groups of people as victims in need of protection from criticism, and which makes believers feel that no dissent should be tolerated.*"

Political correctness, in the end, is a form of attack on a person's freedom to *reason*. I recall years ago when I was in public high school; the Biology teacher was a great guy and a truly gifted teacher. He was also an evolutionist and he taught evolution in the classroom. But what I always appreciated about him was the fact that he never felt obligated to force a student to give up his own beliefs about Creation itself. In fact, I recall on an exam that he simply wanted us to be able to explain – without necessarily believing – the nature of evolution. We were also free to discuss our own understanding of Creationism.

That does not happen today. In fact, if you believe God created the heavens and the earth in six twenty-four-hour periods you're an unenlightened idiot. Just ask Richard Dawkins. He has little to no patience for those who do not see the "facts" of Evolution. It wasn't always like that in school. Students were free to voice their ideas and ask questions, but not today.

It is clear that Browne understands the situation facing society today, as do many of those he quotes in his book. I'll end this chapter with one more quote from him.

*"The rise of political correctness represents an assault on both reason and liberal democracy. It is an assault on reason, because the measuring stick of the acceptability of a belief is no longer its objective, empirically established truth, but how well it fits in with the received wisdom of political correctness. It is an assault on liberal democracy, because the pervasiveness of political correctness is closing down freedom of speech and open debate."*

# Chapter 8
# Dumbing It Down

Today's individual is all too often bound by unwritten laws and policy derived from political correctness, which tends to act as a millstone around the neck. While we are going through life we have this strong sense that if we say the wrong word or give the wrong look we could not only find ourselves on the receiving end of society's ire, but we may also be forced to the outer edges of society as well. This type of affront to our rational mind leaves us feeling as though we have fallen down the rabbit hole. How could this be happening, we wonder?

I think Anthony Browne summarizes it best. "*For the modern mind, confronted with a new set of policy options on a difficult issue, the first reaction is not to try and divine the right answer, but the 'politically-correct' one. Many people will think first of what the true answer is, and in an effort to avoid controversy or offence (sic), measure it up against the dictates of political correctness. Those whose intellectual faculties have been all but closed down by political correctness have learnt (sic) to automatically short-cut to the PC response.*" - Anthony Browne, The Retreat of Reason

In essence, being politically correct is for *cowards*. It is the easy way out so that a person is not seen as offensive to others. It is the epitome of someone who is pusillanimous and therefore fully reprehensible. No wonder God views it as compromising with the world, because just as Adam and Eve sided with Satan against God in Eden, people are tempted to compromise with the world daily because they are so afraid of being ostracized by that world. To God, compromise with the world is *anathema*.

Take for example the instance when the owner of Chick-Fil-A stated – in response to a question posed to him – he believes homosexuality is wrong, according to the Bible. What happened? The gay and lesbian community went nuts, doing everything they could to paint a picture of Mr. Cathy as a virulent hater and one who should be fully censured. They did what they could to vilify him, creating an image of him as the lowest of low. In other words, if a Christian has an opinion that happens to agree with Scripture regarding (in this case) homosexuality, we should keep it to ourselves or risk the rage and indignation of gay and lesbian groups.

How was this accomplished by the politically correct Left? They attacked Chick-Fil-A through boycotting, vandalizing, and through their own use of "hate speech." However, since gay and lesbian groups are within the arena of political correctness (they are seen as "victims"), nothing they do or say is seen as wrong. They or those who sympathize with them can vandalize the side of a Chick-Fil-A restaurant and people outwardly side with that individual. After all, it is believed, the "hatred" that is evidenced by Dan Cathy cannot go unpunished because he is seen as the "aggressor."

The same thing happened with Kirk Cameron, who appeared on the Piers Morgan TV show. Morgan blindsided Cameron by asking him what he thought about same-sex marriage. Though Cameron was put on the spot, he remained true to the biblical teaching that homosexuality is wrong. Certainly, God does not condone it, no more than He condones sex outside of marriage or adultery or prostitution.

What was the response to Cameron's honest remarks? It was seen in abject hatred from the politically correct Left, who believed that it was perfectly fine to "hate" Cameron (the aggressor) for voicing his honest opinion about what the Bible teaches. The hatred that is constantly on display from those within the politically correct crowd is generally accepted by society because, after all, gays and lesbians are "victims," and that gives them the right to push back against the "aggressor."

It's cowardly the way adherents of political correctness make the rules. They make them in a way that props *them* up while making anyone who has a dissenting viewpoint to be seen as a "hater."

Most celebs now who are asked about the homosexual lifestyle react in a cowardly way by simply presenting a response that makes the PC-police happy. Some, like Carrie Underwood, are Christian, yet it is clear to me that Jesus would not simply stand on the sidelines and say something like, "*Oh, I cannot imagine what it would be like to not be able to marry anyone I chose to marry*" or some such nonsense. The truth of the matter is that if asked, He would likely point out the problem, whether it was politically correct to do so or not.

The overriding issue has to do with the fact that people *want* to be accepted today. They want to be seen as loving and accepting of others. Because they prefer to receive a high-five from the world (as opposed to hearing "*Well done!*" from God), they are willing to entertain all sorts of compromises. The saddest part of it is that many of these "Christians" have (in my opinion) compromised their witness for Christ by catering to the world's view of something, but then they go beyond this to attack others who believe that they are standing on the Word. This is compromise.

The other day, in response to one of my articles on my blog[39], I received an email from a young man who states he is a Christian and also a Leftist. He is studying for ministry and looks forward to serving the Lord when he has completed his studies. The fact that he is a Leftist makes no sense to me. As a response, he wrote this:

> "If for you 'Christian' means gun-toting, Constitution worshipping, patriotic idolatry, gay hating, anti-science, anti-fact, 6,000 year old earth, static, unchanging, antiquated, ignorant, misunderstanding and misusing the term 'Marxist,' biblical literalism, rapture horse manure, and broad sweeping claims about people you obviously have never had an intelligent conversation with...then yes, we use the term differently.
>
> "Your posts would be comical if I thought you were joking, but it seems you really believe the garbage you tout."

He's been reading my articles for quite some time, so he really *should* know what my definition of being a Christian is since I have discussed it so often. However, please note that what he has done in his response is something that anyone within the politically correct arena does. He attacks in an attempt to belittle, frustrate, castigate, and

---

[39] http://www.studygrowknowblog.com

eventually completely shut down. It is clear that he is not interested in dialogue at all. He simply wants to impose his viewpoint on mine through verbal assault.

Notice the number of points he mirrors, which are often key points that emanate from the Left and politically correct. He accuses me of being a "gun-toter." The ramifications of the label are obvious. It means that, as a Christian, I should not rely on a gun to keep myself or my family safe. That's his opinion, but there is nothing in Scripture that keeps me from using lethal force to defend myself if necessary. In fact, there are numerous sections that support it.

Then, he moves on to another area that really riles politically correct individuals. He accuses me of worshiping the Constitution, which of course is not true. As I pointed out to him, I merely *respect* the founding documents as the rule of law in this country, understanding what the founders went through in order to create America.

He accuses me of patriotic idolatry, which ties in with the previous attack on the Constitution. Unfortunately for him, he is confusing respecting something with idolatry.

He next calls me a hater of gays. He doesn't even know me. He is not aware that my wife and I have gay friends. In fact, we have been there for a particular lesbian couple who have adopted a young boy and experienced difficulties in that process. They know we love them, though they also know that we do not agree with their lifestyle. We certainly don't condemn them for it and they know it.

Moreover, when my wife and I married (about twenty-seven years ago), one of my friends – who happened to be gay – was part of my wedding party. I don't hate gays, any more than I hate the young man who wrote the email.

But this is what those within the politically correct arena do. To them, it is cut and dry. They are programmed to believe that people like me hate gays or worship the Constitution. This gives them grounds to react as they do, which is devoid of *reason* and based solely on *emotion*. It is all from the belly, built on their very strong emotion. It has nothing to do with clear thinking or logical reasoning. They *have* to hate the person they are attempting to destroy. It is impossible for them to have a sane conversation with those who stand opposed to their ideas and beliefs.

Can Chris Matthews, Ed Schultz, or Lawrence O'Donnell have a sane conversation about or with someone who is not part of the politically correct arena? They can't do it. They always resort to a focused, emotional attack on the person they believe is a hater. It's not reasoned by any stretch.

This is why Joe Biden acted as he did during his debate with Sen. Paul Ryan. There was no sense of civility at all emanating from Biden. He acted the buffoon in many ways. No decorum.

Because he is part of the politically correct crowd, he is encouraged and expected to act as he did and he gets a pass because of his politically correct viewpoints. Paul Ryan would not have gotten away with it had he reacted as Biden did during the same debate.

political correctness has infiltrated every area of society, especially the media. It will only stop when we start resisting it by ignoring it and simply being ourselves.

We need to take our thought lives back from the PC police. We need to be able to speak our minds without worrying about whether some person within the politically correct arena is going to shout us down and verbally reprimand and attempt to censure us.

political correctness makes it fashionable (and expected) to shout down and attempt to embarrass those who hold a different (even though valid) opinion on something. People desperately want to be accepted by others so they will say what is expected of them in order to be accepted. Who wants to be ostracized?

This kind of demeanor is what Jesus spoke *against*. A person who practices this type of compromising shows that his self-worth is more valuable to him than God's truth.

A few years ago, when Butterball decided to use the Islamic Halal process in the production of all their turkeys, it created quite a stir. The shame of it is that it was done as a form of subterfuge. Unlike Kosher foods, there is nothing on Halal food packaging that indicates the turkey went through the Halal process at all.

When it *did* come to light, people were very upset, and we had no problem stating our minds on Butterball's social network page. What was very interesting, though, was to see others who said they were Christians and who were just so glad that now *"everyone could enjoy a Butterball turkey."* Others chimed in to shut down the conversation by making those of us who disagreed with the surreptitious nature used by Butterball feel stupid. It didn't work.

Butterball can do anything they want to do. It's their business. They had chosen to use the Halal process for all their turkeys, not just some of them. What's wrong with that, you might ask? It immediately shut out orthodox Jews, who would not be able to eat a Butterball turkey any longer because the turkeys were not Kosher. So much for the claim that everyone allegedly can now eat a Butterball turkey.

But what amazed me are the names that I and others of like mind were called by these "Christians" who disagreed with our position. Butterball could have done something to truly make everyone happy by offering some of their turkeys one way, having undergone the Halal process, and some another way, not having gone through the Halal process. This would have allowed everyone to enjoy their turkeys and actually have a choice. Instead, Butterball chose to cater to *one* group, automatically eliminating another.

I'm tired of being expected to cater to gays, Islam, or anyone else. I do *not* hate people, regardless of their religion, creed, or ethnicity, but I *do* hate political correctness.

I'm tired of being accused of hating people by simpletons who continually fall back, not on the truth of Scripture, but on the relativism of political correctness. It needs to stop and it will only stop when people stand up for their rights and freedoms and stop kowtowing to those on the Left who believe that political correctness somehow equals absolute truth. It doesn't.

*Reject* political correctness. Take back your mind.

*Falling Away*

# Chapter 9
# Politically Correct Christianity

The more I learn about the problem of political correctness, the more I realize it has absolutely no place in the life of an *authentic* Christian. None. Zero. Zilch.

The very nature of political correctness forces a person to compromise what they know (or *should* know) is the truth. Is this what Paul is referring to when he speaks of the *darkening of a person's mind* in Romans 1:21-23? When society comes to a point of acting, speaking, and even thinking based on a set of unwritten rules that are often juxtaposed against God and His Word, then that society has truly lost its way. When people who claim to be Christians also get carried away by it, they bring dishonor to the Name of Christ, their alleged Lord.

We live in a world culture that is growing in its resentment to orthodox Christianity. Those of us who believe that salvation is specifically found in and due to Jesus' life, death, and resurrection and is only available directly through Him are becoming anathema to those in the world. They don't want to hear it. They become inordinately angry when they hear about the need for a person to be saved through repentance and gratefully receive salvation in Christ.

Too many alleged Christian leaders, ministers, and authors talk about ways to salvation which to some degree circumvent Jesus Christ. Of course, they deny that charge, but if we can know them by what they write and say, then we can know whether or not what they teach is truth or simply another version of New Age mentality wrapped in religious garb.

You know, Jesus made some extremely startling and even demanding statements to the people of His day, which are recorded for us in Scripture. People were literally shocked and, in a few cases, were shocked enough to stop following Him altogether. More than anything, He told people that if they were *unwilling* to take up their crosses and follow Him they were not worthy of Him. At least the people of Jesus' day had the integrity to walk away from Him when they found they could not agree with Him.

In today's world, people don't really stop following Him. They simply *redefine* Christianity to their liking so that it's much more comfortable and easier to wear so that it doesn't chafe them. They change what Jesus said so that His words become more palatable. They use all manner of faulty reasoning (such as it is) to allow them to make Christianity more appetizing to the masses, yet it has no ability to save or change anyone. In the end, it becomes seriously watered down pabulum in their hands and then they have the nerve to claim that that's what Jesus *really* meant.

In the end though, Jesus placed very high demands on His followers, and not long after His own ascension that commitment was tried – literally – by fire for many Christians with Nero. I cannot help but wonder how many Christians would go willingly to their deaths today because of their commitment to Christ.

Jesus tells us that the world hated Him and this same world will also hate us. Yet there are so many "Christians" living in ease and comfort, aren't there? They only speak of things that are "politically correct" because doing so keeps them out of trouble with the world. While they're trying to please the world, they have unfortunately rejected the Lord who has saved them.

When the world begins to circle the wagons menacingly around them, political correctness comes to their rescue! *"Well, look, we don't want to offend people, so I'll just keep to myself. I'll let my life speak for itself so that people will see Christ in me. That is what will change them!"* Sure, why not? Jesus just *lived* a life, didn't He? He never really *said* anything to people, nor did He ever really take the time to *explain* things. He never got into arguments with the religious leaders and He certainly never deigned to tell the common person what they were doing wrong. That would have been offensive. No, He just did things that showed how much He loved people.

Obviously, Jesus *did* things for people. He healed the sick. He raised the dead. He fed thousands. Of course, the most important thing He did was to offer His life as a propitiation for the sins of humanity. He died a horribly brutal death, shedding His blood on our behalf, and then He rose from the dead. His actions obviously spoke (and continue to speak) of love, didn't they?

But He was also a man of *words,* and too often His words put Him at odds with the politically correct parasites of His day: the religious leaders and even the average person. Yet He did not pull Himself back. He did not couch His words so that those people would not be offended. He said what He said because it was truth! Absolute truth by its very nature has the ability to offend. I am speaking of God's truth here, not some man-made pabulum that allegedly has the crux of truth but is nothing more than relativism that changes like the wind.

Today, we have a plethora of religious leaders who tell us lies about the Bible. They fill their own plate with contemptible tidbits of what they try to pass off as truth. Everything they say is couched in politically correct verbiage. Oh no, we mustn't say something that might offend. That would push the people away from Christ. Would it?

Then how is it that so many were saved because they did not find the gospel offensive, yet they were told just how sinful they were in reality? In Acts 2, Peter gives his very first sermon after the Holy Spirit rained Himself down on the 120 believers in the Upper Room. What was the response? While some muttered, made fun, and ridiculed, 3,000 came to know the Lord that day! Peter held nothing back. He let go with both barrels, telling people how sinful they had been, just like their forefathers, and how through unbelief they were kept from knowing God. That was their decision, not God's.

Yet, while the truth that Peter spoke brought 3,000 into God's Kingdom that day, many others balked at the exact same truth! Why? Because they refused to acknowledge that their politically correct ways were killing them, slowly yet steadily.

When Rick Warren gave the invocation at Mr. Obama's first inaugural event in 2008, Warren specifically used the word *"Isa"* in reference to Jesus during his prayer. Why? Because he wanted to be politically correct by reaching out to Muslims in the process. He also wanted to be seen as a man whom others could look up to and honor. "*Oh, look at Rick Warren! He spoke of Jesus in our terms! What a good man Rick Warren is!*"

Never mind that by using the word "*Isa*" to reference Jesus, Warren also *lowered* the nature and position of Jesus to a point *below* Muhammad's. This is the way Muslims think of Jesus: He is an important historical figure, but Jesus is most decidedly below Muhammad. While Muslims certainly respect Jesus, they do not see Him nor accept Him as God the Son. But here's the thing: Jesus is not asking for our respect!

Jesus asks for our all, our very life, because He gave us His! He asks and demands that we become His indentured slaves, willingly, because we love Him, not out of any sense of duty. But too many people who call themselves Christians care more about what the world thinks about them. Jesus isn't physically here, walking beside them or instructing them. The world is, and so the temptations to cater to the world and cave into its demands are too much for too many. This is so tragic it is beyond words.

These types of Christians "do" a lot of things in Jesus's Name, but could these individuals be the very ones that Jesus claims to have never known in Matthew 7? People who cater to the world cannot also cater to God. When Jesus said you cannot serve God and Mammon (money), He meant exactly that. But He also meant that when two things pull at your heart, you will give in to only one of them. A person cannot have a divided loyalty.

If you find yourself going along with the people in the world because you have somehow convinced yourself that *"God will understand that I'm only trying to 'love' these people,"* then you are, unfortunately, seriously deluded. Where in Scripture did Jesus ever compromise with the world system? When did He ever attempt to placate the world though doing so meant not honoring His Father? How can we – how can I – treat Jesus in such a despicable manner? How?

I'm not saying we go through life with a death wish or a persecution complex of our own making. I'm saying that Jesus was a man of sorrows and acquainted with grief. He knew what it was to be deserted by friends and family. He knew what it meant to be threatened with death while innocent of any and all wrongdoing. Jesus knew the sorrow of betrayal.

Yet in all these things He never once gave in to the temptation to please the world in order that the world might think of Him as one swell guy! He never gave the world the opportunity for that and this is exactly what He expects of those of us who claim to be His followers – nothing less.

We cannot compromise with the world through political correctness. It will shut us down and destroy our testimony. If we give in to political correctness, we are saying "no" to God; no, we won't follow you here. No, we will not speak the truth there. No, you are not our Lord in that situation.

We either take our calling seriously, endeavoring in all things to live for Christ regardless of the reproach the world heaps on us because of it, or we stop telling people that we are "Christian." It is that simple. Either we are *for* God, or we stand *opposed* to Him.

In the last hours of His life, Jesus was alone. He had no one. All had left Him, and even the Father turned His back on Jesus in rejection as the Father's wrath poured over Jesus because He who knew no sin became sin for us (2 Corinthians 5:21).

Pick up your cross every day. Understand that the same world system that hated Jesus will also hate you. If the world loves you, you are doing something terribly wrong. Bow before Him and His majesty. Claim Him as your King. Put Him as Lord in every situation so that He will work in and through you to accomplish His will.

Brothers and sisters in Christ, we must pray for one another that the evil one gains no footing in our lives. We must cast off the works of darkness (cf. Romans 13:12), of which political correctness is chief. It masquerades as truth, while it is nothing more than lies heaped on top of lies. Walk away from it. Treat it as if it is the worst social disease you can imagine.

Walk in truth at every turn. Endeavor to please Him, not the world. If you are a Christian, then you cannot live by the thorny and deceptive rules of a politically correct world.

# Chapter 10
# Politically Correct Noah

014. The Prophecy of the Flood
Genesis. Chapter 6, Verses 13–22.

I have read a good deal by many about what Noah's day was like, as well as about what Lot's day was like and what we can expect in the End Times (times I believe we are now living in). Jesus mentions the people of Noah's day in His Olivet Discourse of Matthew 24, Mark 13, and Luke 21. It is definitely worth our time to understand just exactly what Jesus was referring to.

When Jesus referenced the days of Noah as well as the days of Lot, was he talking mainly about fallen angels who found a way to procreate with human women (days of Noah)? It would seem that since

Jesus points to both the days of Noah as well as the days of Lot as being similar to the way it would be just prior to the end of this age, then maybe He was actually referring to something else.

We need to remember that Jesus was pointing out the *similarities* regarding both Noah's day and Lot's day, and He used those examples as situations that would also exist during the time of the end, the time just prior to His future physical return. There is no mention or reference to Nephilim in Lot's situation.

In Genesis 19, we are introduced to two of the angels who had already spent time with Abraham. In Genesis 18, there were three individuals, one of whom we believe to be a pre-incarnate appearance of Jesus. During that time the Lord spoke to Abraham, explaining what would take place with respect to Sodom and Gomorrah. Both cities were scheduled to be destroyed.

Abraham became concerned because his nephew Lot and his family lived in Sodom. Through a series of questions and answers, God assured Abraham that He would not destroy those cities if only as few as ten righteous people lived there. Unfortunately, as we are to learn, only Lot and his two daughters escaped the destruction.

Genesis 19 opens with the angelic messengers having just arrived at the gate of Sodom, where Lot sat. It was close to evening and it was the time for most people to head inside. Of course, we learn in a few moments that not everyone went inside, but many actually came outside during this time of the evening. That's normal for most cities. However, Lot grew concerned about the welfare of the two visiting individuals. I doubt at this point that Lot understood they were angels. If so, he probably would not have been so concerned for their safety.

The text is very clear that Lot asks them to "turn aside" and stay with him in his home (v. 2). The men say they will "*spend the night in the square*" (v. 2b). Lot becomes concerned, as we see in verse three where he urges them strongly to go with him to his home. Lot clearly did not think it safe for them to remain out-of-doors during the night. Finally, they acquiesce to Lot. Some cities today are also like that, or at least parts of them are, where it's not good to go outside at night.

Verse four then tells us that the men – both old and young – of the town came to Lot's home and surrounded it. Genesis 19:5 states that the men ask, "*Where are the men who came to you tonight? Bring them out to us that we may have relations with them.*"

Other translations say the men wanted to "know" the strangers. It is clearly a sexual reference, and anyone who would deny this is kidding himself and proving his ignorance. The men wanted to have sex with these two strangers, whether the two strangers wanted to participate willingly or not. Though many possible explanations of the "true" meaning of this passage have been offered, it is unmistakably clear that the men wanted to know the two strangers in a sexual way.

The Politically Correct Police have done everything they can to ensure that this section of Scripture does not reflect badly on homosexuality. It wouldn't do to have people think that there were homosexuals alive during Lot's day who wanted to rape two male strangers, even if those are the facts.

It is clear that Lot knew what the men of the town wanted because he offers his own two virgin daughters to the men and boys of Sodom in the hopes that this will satisfy them and they will leave the two male strangers alone. I would not have offered what Lot offered at all. The fact that Lot made it clear that his daughters were virgins also contextually confirms the fact that the men were interested in having sex with these two visitors. It is too clear to deny, yet people do deny it because they don't like what it says or the ramifications of it.

Let me state – clearly – that sin is sin. I'm a sinner and so are you. Jesus points out in the Sermon on the Mount of Matthew 5–7 that to lust after a person is the same thing as participating in a sexual liaison with them physically. To God, there is no difference at all. Socially, the stigma and consequences of our physical sin may be greater than our mental sin (e.g. sexually transmitted diseases, pregnancy, divorce, etc.), but there is no difference between the thought (lust) and the physical act (sex) as far as God is concerned.

But the Politically Correct Police of today come along and deny the obvious meaning of Genesis 19. They decide that we cannot have this in the Bible about homosexuals because it makes homosexuals look bad. Therefore, they attempt to change the meaning, yet they fail miserably at every turn. So they opt to simply deny the truth, as if all homosexuals are above the desire to rape someone or to take sexual advantage of a child. I see, so they are super humans, huh? Right.

By the same token, I'm quite certain there are many homosexuals today who do not think of raping other men, but there are probably some homosexuals today who think of it a lot. There are men who think of raping women all the time as well, but certainly not all men. Why should we eliminate any reference to actions of depraved homosexuals that occur in the Bible but leave the examples of adultery, rape, or murder done by heterosexuals? Do homosexuals expect us to believe that they are all above raping another individual as happened in Lot's day? Apparently. Such a fairy tale.

As an aside, you know that show "To Catch a Predator" in which Chris Hansen sets up an elaborate scheme to catch male predators going after young girls? They reel them in one after another, and thank God for that if it gets these people off the streets.

But why don't we ever see an episode about men wanting to have sex with young boys? I have yet to see an episode about that. If an episode exists, I haven't seen it and don't even know of it.

Perverted Justice is a force behind the show and they do a great deal to catch pedophiles. But do they actively pursue male pedophiles who go after young boys, or are they only interested in male pedophiles who go after young girls? I've written to the individuals at Perverted Justice twice and have yet to receive a response.

Truth is, if Chris Hansen's TV show went after men who preferred underage boys as sex toys, we might expect to hear loud complaints from gay activists. Obviously, they really don't want us to see homosexuality as "normal." They want us to see homosexuals as supernormal, without any sexual flaws. Isn't a pedophile a pedophile, regardless of their gender preference?

There are likely homosexuals who want a solid relationship with one other person. The homosexuals living in Lot's city were apparently not like that. They had one thing on their mind and that's what they wanted. Still, it is clear from God's Word that homosexuality is wrong. It is not what God created or intended. It is not part of His ordered universe. It is the result of fallen humanity.

If He had wanted it, don't you think He would have made provision for it in the Garden of Eden? But of course, here is another place where the Politically Correct Police come to laugh you to scorn if you deign to be stupid enough to believe that God created Adam and Eve. Of course it didn't happen like that, they charge! It's a metaphor; a fanciful story!

But getting back to the story, we read that the men of the town rejected Lot's offer with the words, *"This one came in as an alien, and already he is acting like a judge; now we will treat you worse than them"* (Genesis 19:9). By the way, just so we're clear here, the word "alien" is not referring to either beings from outer space or illegal aliens that flood into this country from places like Mexico. In this context, the word "alien" simply means "stranger" from another land, and Lot's presence in Sodom was not illegal or from outer space. I add this as a courtesy to those who like to claim that people like myself really don't take Scripture literally. My earnest endeavor is to understand Scripture as God intended, so yes, I try to glean the literal meaning of Scripture at every turn, just as I do in everyday speech with people.

So the threats begin from the militant men of the crowd. They have no patience for Lot or his sanctimonious and judgmental attitude. Just whom does Lot think he is anyway, and who made him boss? They will now treat him much more brutally than the two visitors when they have finished with them. Nice, isn't it? You have to love the Left, don't you? They will do whatever they can to shut down anyone with whom they disagree, even if it includes, in this case, physical brutality. Obviously, Lot – a hater – had it coming to him.

But here is my question. How did Lot's society get to that point, where homosexuals ran around doing whatever they wanted to do to people without restraint? How did that happen? The same way it happened during Noah's day.

It happened because they were able to, over a considerable amount of time, reject any semblance of absolute right and wrong in Sodom and Gomorrah. It didn't happen overnight but over the long haul, until finally these men literally took over Sodom and Gomorrah, doing whatever it was they wanted. They had become the politically correct militants of their time and forced their wills upon the people of the cities. Obviously, no one was able to stop them.

Unbelief through political correctness ultimately has terrible consequences. It is a gradual slide into degradation, and Paul outlines this downward slide for us in the very first chapter of Romans. Starting with verse eighteen, Paul states without hesitation that God's wrath is poured out onto those who cover up the truth by the way they live their lives. That's the way it starts: by a lie that replaces the truth.

Lot was unwilling to play the PC-game. He stood up to the PC-militants of his day as I believe we should in our day. The twin cities of Sodom and Gomorrah were destroyed, though Lot escaped that destruction. That's the end result of aligning ourselves with political correctness: a terrible compromise with the world system that always ends badly. The world may think you're a swell person, but God will reject you because you have ultimately rejected Him and His truth, having compromised and aligned yourself with the world.

In the end, it's not the world that will judge you regarding eternity. God does that. Doesn't it make more sense to ensure that He is pleased with your actions?

Oh, by the way, in both cases – the days of Noah and the days of Lot – God took Noah and Lot out of the way before He poured out His judgment. It is a picture of the Rapture when God takes His Church out of the way prior to pouring out His judgment onto the earth in the coming days of the Tribulation. But that is another article.

This example of Lot's society and how people change truth into lies and vice versa is merely one example. In future chapters, we will look at other examples of how the politically correct do their best to force people into silence through name-calling and even physical assault when they believe it is warranted (or they can get away with it).

In either case, there are too many people who claim to be Christians who are willing to join in with the Politically Correct Police of society. Let's face it, it's easier.

## Chapter 11
# Politically Correct Protesting

**H**ere is an interesting situation, one that clearly highlights the *illegal* antics of those who are firmly planted within the *politically correct arena.* In a video[40] on the net, you can see two pro-Israeli individuals who were quietly protesting a terrorist organization – Hamas – by writing things in chalk on the sidewalk.

If you take the time to view the video, you'll see that the trouble all starts when one young woman takes umbrage at what the young pro-Israeli girl is writing on the ground in Hebrew. The individual who

---

[40] http://www.youtube.com/watch?v=gpZYMQVO9aw&feature=player_embedded (03/15/2013)

began the altercation is Gabby Silverman, whose mug shot is on the net[41] because apparently Gabby has had previous run-ins with the police.

Be warned that should you choose to watch the video, you may wish to turn the volume down or off completely because young Gabby possesses knowledge of the "F" word and likes to use it. On her social network page, she later gives an account of what transpired.[42]

In her version, she indicates that the two young pro-Israelis were writing *over* the names of Gabby's friends and comrades, which is absolutely not true (unless they actually erased the names first). It's as if Gabby and her buds believe that there is not enough room for dissenting opinions within earshot or eyesight of their own. Oh wait, that's *exactly* what they believe because that's one of the main, unwritten tenets of *political correctness*. No dissenting opinions allowed.

As you watch the video, you will see – quite clearly, in fact – that Gabby has a problem with the young pro-Israeli woman writing on the ground. Gabby's consternation causes her to express her disdain *verbally*, but of course, that's not enough. Soon, she is *physically* pushing and shoving the young woman, repeatedly telling her to "*Get the 'F' out!*" Ah, such tolerance for the opposing opinion. Warms your heart, doesn't it? Can you feel the love?

The young pro-Israeli man tries to intercede by keeping the huffing, puffing, and expletive-shouting Gabby away from the pro-Israeli woman. Then political correctness *really* comes to the fore because

---

[41] http://1.bp.blogspot.com/-qcxhsE51g-4/UUGLrWwO30I/AAAAAAAAFKw/BbjO8xWHj8A/s320/Gabby.jpg (03/15/2013)
[42] http://3.bp.blogspot.com/-c_m1fhgZl4Y/UUPcDbQORbI/AAAAAAAAFLs/MjsxbdrDlN8/s400/gabby.jpg (03/15/2013)

very soon others join in to verbally attack, shove, and essentially shut down the two young pro-Israeli people. Soon the two are literally pushed out of the area, and two security guards enter the picture to break things up. Mission accomplished for political ness. Whew! Another opinion successfully shut down.

Remember, to the politically correct, the Palestinians are seen as "victims" against the "aggression" of Israeli. This is why people can say anti-Semitic things and even attack Israel and those who support them and get away with it. It all boils down to who's the victim and who is classified as the perceived aggressor.

The two young pro-Israeli people shown in the video had *every* right to say what they wanted to say. In fact, they had just as much right to express themselves as the anti-Israeli forces had to express their view. Had the situation been reversed and two young pro-Israeli people started physically attacking people who were anti-Israeli, they would have been just as wrong in their actions.

It's the same with anything. SNL has a right to portray a terrible attempt at satire by doing a skit called "*DeJesus Uncrossed*" and I have every right to voice my dissent over it and to even boycott the companies who support SNL. They have their rights and I have mine. I do *not* have a right to get physically violent with anyone over the issue though. That breaks the law and we are warned throughout the New Testament alone to *support* the rule of law.

Ultimately, Gabby Silverman and her buds are guilty of infringing on the rights of the two pro-Israeli people, not to mention physically assaulting one of them. The latter is an arrestable offense, which the politically correct wear like a badge of honor.

This is what it comes down to for the politically correct. In essence, only *their* opinion is valid and should be allowed to air. Opposing opinions should *not* be aired. Society has come to the point where the politically correct appear to hold more sway than those who are considered to be outside the arena of the politically correct camp. In essence, they are holding the rest of us hostage, and that should not be.

In yet another example of misguided political correctness, a verdict was handed down in the Stuebenville rape trial. Two young men, star football players and good students by the names of Trent Mays and Ma'lik Richmond, were found guilty of rape. Their lives are ruined, but some would like us to believe the fault lies with the *victims*, not the perpetrators. These guys had no criminal past. They're not gangstas. They're "good" young men.

What should be at the very least startling to people is the amount of sympathy that is being extended to these two young men. CNN got into the act (since when is CNN more interested in truth than in political correctness?) with Candy Crowley (yes, *that* Candy Crowley, from the third presidential debate in which she, as moderator, went to bat for Obama against Romney in spite of the rules that prohibited it. Rules do not apply to the politically correct).

In the CNN video, the main thing that sticks out is the sympathy evidenced primarily for the *perpetrators* of the crime. There is really nothing here that extends any real sympathy for the women, who were, let's not forget, the victims in this case. If not for political correctness, I would not understand this at all. But knowing what I know about how political correctness has made good evil and evil good, it is now very clear and simple to comprehend.

If we are to believe CNN, the only thing to talk about here is how the lives of these two young men are over. Apparently, there are plenty *outside* of CNN who are also willing to blame the victims (like those who tweeted things like "*The Steubenville story is all too familiar. Be responsible for your actions ladies before your drunken decisions ruin innocent lives"* and *"So you got drunk at a party and two people take advantage of you, that's not rape you're just a loose drunk slut"*).[43]

Wow, people still think like that today and that's *okay*? Somehow, it's the *woman's* fault? Where are the *feminists* to stand up for the women victims here, or is that only when they need to find someone like Sandra Fluke to complain that she has to pay for her own birth control? Apparently, taxpayers are supposed to pay for that. Now *that's* something feminists can get behind!

The politically correct go after the victims because they are seen as the "aggressors" here. The young men, who had their whole lives in front of them, are the victims to these people. I have to wonder if as much sympathy would have been generated if *both* young men were white? Political correctness would dictate that if both perpetrators were white, then no, there should be no sympathy toward them because white males are generally understood to be "aggressors." Since one of the young men is black, then pity extends to him because he was simply trying to better himself but was struck down by two young women "sluts."

However, at least one female blogger, after watching the CNN report, immediately took to the blogosphere to send a message of her own. She understood the situation and stated, *"Their dreams and hopes were not crushed by an impersonal, inexorable legal system; Mays and Richardson raped a girl and have been sentenced accordingly,"* and this one: *"Reporting like this presents viewers with anonymous female victims and dynamic, sympathetic, complicated male figures."*[44]

---

[43] http://www.theatlanticwire.com/national/2013/03/cnns-not-only-one-peddling-sympathy-steubenville-rapists/63204/ (03/22/2013)
[44] http://www.theatlanticwire.com/national/2013/03/cnns-not-only-one-peddling-sympathy-steubenville-rapists/63204/ (03/22/2013)

This mentality is something that feminists have long fought *against*, that women are *not* somehow to blame if men take advantage of them. The old saying "*she was asking for it*" was thought to have gone the way of the dinosaur, but I guess it's back and given new respectability if the victims in the case (the young girls) can be made to be seen as the "aggressors."

Here's the truth, which may be hard for some to accept: even if a woman walks down the street *nude*, she is *not* asking for it. She may get arrested for being nude in public, but she is not necessarily *asking* for someone to rape her.

Men do not have the "right" to molest or rape a woman because *to them* it appears as though she is *asking* for it. A woman "asks" for it when she actually *consents willingly* to a sexual liaison. Anything less than that constitutes the crime of *rape*, regardless of what many men (and even some women) prefer to believe.

Justice has done its job in this case. If the verdict is wrong and these young men were unfairly found guilty, then they need new lawyers and a retrial. Hopefully they will have opportunity to prove their innocence if they are, in fact, innocent. However, at least one of the perpetrators offered what may certainly have been a heartfelt apology for his actions, ending with tears and an inability to finish his apology to the victim. If he wasn't guilty, why was he apologizing over what he had done, especially considering what he said to the victim during his apology?

The young men's lives *have* taken a turn for the worse. Whose fault is that? Apparently, in CNN's politically correct world, the young female victims are to blame.

God holds the young men fully accountable for their actions. God doesn't check with Candy Crowley or CNN before arriving at His inviolate decision. All of God's judgments are based on justice, reason, and truth, not *political correctness* or the changing motif of emotional virtue.

The fact that these young women were victimized not once (when the rapes first occurred) but a second time in the social media and in the news is testament to the fact that political correctness has captured America and shows little signs of letting go. However, it *needs* to go, and people who understand the difference between absolute right and wrong should be the ones who help it go away permanently.

It amazes me how often those within the *politically correct arena* actually believe they are intellectually superior to those outside of the PC-arena. The name-calling, the labeling, the shouting: it's all such a joke, but it so easily builds their tiny, frail egos.

Unfortunately, they simply do not realize how foolish they often sound (and that's putting it nicely). So Candy Crowley and other CNN reporters take time out to sympathize with the men who were actually found guilty of raping young women? They *raped* women! How does Crawley live with herself? She is obviously only concerned about keeping her job, not dispensing the truth.

Or take Gabby Silverman, who believes it is perfectly fine to shut down someone with whom she disagrees, effectively removing their right to free speech. I have no problem with Silverman saying what she wants to say or using chalk to write what she wants. She has that right under the same Constitution that also guarantees the right of others to *disagree* with her. She has *no* right to *attempt to take away* another's right to express herself using the same freedom of speech simply because Silverman doesn't like the message. That's tyrannical demagoguery and it's what the PC-police are so good at these days.

These people end up continually fulfilling Romans 1:22, where Paul tells us that they are ultimately fools, merely pretending (and believing themselves) to be wise. They're not wise. They are the opposite, but they fail to see it because they believe they are part of something that sets them above everyone else.

Maybe people are starting to wake up. Some appear to be taking the time to resist this type of mental and emotional tyranny. Maybe they're getting sick and tired of the pretentiousness and falseness of political correctness, which hides the truth at every turn, replacing the truth with nothing but lies. Certainly God will end it one day, but I believe authentic Christians have an obligation to resist it now as well. Too many don't because it is much easier to go along with the world because of all the "high-fives" they receive in the process.

Maybe people are coming round to realize that political correctness, no matter how well-intentioned it was at the start, has become a millstone around the necks of civilized and intelligent people. If that realization has started taking root in good people, that's a good thing.

*Falling Away*

# Chapter 12
# Political Correctness on Parade!

There are some interesting videos that I'm referencing in this chapter that highlight situations that have fast become the norm. In the first one, a military vet is seen in handcuffs and being led away from what turns out to be a pro-union rally.[45] In another video,[46] this same man is seen at the rally holding some signs and bothering no one. He is first ordered by the police to stand in one place. When he asks why he has to do that and raises his arm to

---

[45] http://www.youtube.com/watch?feature=player_embedded&v=rEb2gEFIDQo (03/26/2013)
[46] https://www.youtube.com/watch?v=i3s4R4b-k74 (03/26/2013)

point to another place where he had been standing, the officer places him in cuffs. The crowd goes wild.

In another video,[47] he is being led away and he cannot get an answer from officers as to why he is being arrested. He was, as he states, simply *peacefully* protesting, and there is plenty of video footage to prove it. Apparently, though, since it was a union rally, that created some problems because the union people didn't like his message or his presence.

When he is finally taken away, the crowd goes wild, shouting that he should be taken to jail, etc. There certainly may be extenuating circumstances on another video that shows he broke the law, but I can't find that video if it exists.

Please also note as the man attempts to claim his Constitutional right to peacefully protest (and is promptly ignored), many of the union people start shouting him down: a favorite tactic of the politically correct crowd. The officers also essentially ignore his pleas for answers. Would it have anything to do with the fact that the officers themselves are likely part of unions?

In another instance, during a Tea Party rally held in Boston, militant Leftists stormed the rally with their slogans, their banners, and their rudeness for one purpose: to drown out the Tea Party speakers and disrupt the rally.[48]

You can see that at one point someone from the Tea Party tries to get the police to intervene, but the police can't be bothered. It should also be noted that in order to have one of these rallies, permits (legal permission) have to be obtained and other preparations have to be made.

---

[47] https://www.youtube.com/watch?v=rE62gEFTDQo (03/26/2013)
[48] https://www.youtube.com/watch?v=CGLSb-8iYp4 (03/26/2013)

In one case when something like this happened, the Tea Party folks even met with the police beforehand and were promised that the police would make sure nothing like this took place. When push comes to shove though, the police *do* simply allow it to happen. Yet with the Occupy Movement, participants there defecated on police cruisers, hurled things at police, people were shot, and at least one rape took place. So the politically correct have their set of rules and those of us who support the rule of law of the land have ours.

In the first example with the military vet, we see him being carted off for breaking no law. He was also shouted down by union people at the rally. While the cameras ran, he was never even told *why* he was being arrested, what law he had broken. I do realize that in some locales, police have so many hours before they inform someone why they are being detained. Moreover, they also do not have to *immediately* read a person their rights in every instance. However, as a courtesy, you would think that the officer would have informed the man, but he chose not to do so.

Here's a question: do you think if the military vet had been a person of color, he would have been treated like that or arrested? If so, what would Sharpton have said or done? How might Obama have weighed in on the situation? Of course, I fully realize that simply asking the very question I just asked is *not* politically correct.

In the second video, we see the exact opposite happen. In that video, members of the Tea Party jumped through all the proper hoops in order to have the rally. In the end, politically correct goons simply ran roughshod over the event because they did not like what the Tea Party was offering and simply wanted to shut them down.

Now, does the union have a right to have a rally? Certainly they do. Had the military vet been creating real problems or broken the law, the police would have had a reason to arrest him. The fact that he was, as the officer stated, "*gonna get [his] a\*\* kicked*" by the crowd is **not** reason enough to arrest him.

If someone *attacked* him because they didn't like his message, *they* should be arrested, not him.  Then again, we saw from a previous chapter how people still believe that women who go to parties and get drunk are "sluts," therefore if they are raped, they apparently had it coming.  I'm sure this same line of thought applies to this man.  They would say if he is stupid enough to go to a union rally, he deserves what he gets.  But that is not what the laws of this land say.  It's what the *politically correct* say and think.

There was an occurrence that took place a year or so ago, people entered into the Arab Festival in Dearborn, MI for the purpose of *evangelizing* Muslims.  These individuals could not be kept out because the festival was on city property and was open to the public.

With the individuals who were intent on evangelizing the Muslims, the Arab attendees became angered and began pelting the first group with rocks, concrete, and some reports even said *urine* was used in the assault.  The police essentially did nothing, though they were right there and *should* have stepped in to stop the attack.  They basically allowed the attackers to do what they wanted to do.

Did the individuals have a right to go into the festival to evangelize?  Sure.  Was it smart?  Not necessarily.  Did Muslims have any sort of right to physically attack the people who were attempting to evangelize them?  No, not at all.  If that's allowable in their home countries, that's one thing.  It's not allowable here in America, yet the police *acted* as if it was within the confines of the law.  Why weren't *the* Muslim perpetrators arrested?  Because the police shirked their duties *and* trampled the man's rights.

This is the way things have gotten throughout parts of America. The constitutional rule of law has been set aside in favor of political correctness, which has replaced the concept of "blind justice" with "judicial favoritism." People who are determined to be victims at some point throughout history are given special privileges.

This is really what the Trayvon Martin/George Zimmerman situation is all about. There have been many documented (but unreported) cases of black on white violence that go nowhere because whites, especially white males, are not seen as true victims *historically*. It is a growing problem in America according to numerous commentators, though dutifully ignored by the political correct Left.

This is also why the Tawana Brawley case from years ago initially caused people to believe her, even though there was not one shred of evidence to support her claims. Likewise, when the Duke Lacrosse scandal came to light, the young (white) males were immediately seen as guilty because of their *privileged* position in society.

This is certainly not to say that accusations should not be seriously considered, but when there is no connecting evidence (as quickly became obvious in the Tawana Brawley and Duke cases), prosecutors need to let go. The particular prosecutor in the Duke case was obviously more interested in making a name for himself on the backs of several innocent young men than in seeing that justice was done. He couldn't drop it and was eventually disbarred as an attorney because of it.[49]

Political correctness creates travesties of justice because it tends to focus inordinately and unfavorably on one group of people bound together by creed, religion, or ethnicity over another person or group due to some type of favoritism. Unfortunately, political correctness

---

[49] http://articles.cnn.com/2007-06-16/justice/duke.lacrosse_1_north-carolina-state-bar-durham-county-district-attorney-mike-nifong?_s=PM:LAW (03/22/2013)

is creating an attitude within society that actually winds up pitting people against other people *because* of race, creed, religion, or gender. It shouldn't be that way, but that is how political correctness works. It does so because it is not guided by absolute truth but by an ever-changing palette of politically correct humanistic *relativism* in which blind *emotion,* not biblical *reasoning,* directs the decision-making process.

## Chapter 13
# Political Correctness Is (Not) Fabulous!

In an ongoing effort by those within the *politically correct arena* to remove all vestiges of traditional values in America, especially those that reflect *biblical* values, PC-militants continually work to facilitate society in making a clean break from anything that smacks of Christianity.

Those with critical thinking skills understand that for the PC-police, Islam is completely off-limits because it had no part in this country's foundation. They also know that if anyone produced some satire like this about Muhammad, his or her life might be in danger – *literally*.

To this end, it has become tantamount that the PC-militants do everything they can to tear down the truth and reality of Christianity. Recently, we learned (from MassResistance.org) that a blasphemous play was produced and offered to the community called "*The Most Fabulous Story Ever Told.*" An image highlighting the play clearly indicates that at least part of the story is about Adam and "Steve."

Now, if you consider yourself a Christian and you find yourself smirking at the idea, then you may wish to question your commitment to Christ. But of course, you likely believe that He would have found this production to be quite entertaining, that He would laugh at His own expense from a front row seat.

Think again, and then maybe you can start by actually reading the Bible as it is written. Save your breath about your erroneous belief that the Bible has been changed and altered throughout the years by unscrupulous scribes who didn't know what they were doing. All of these arguments – such as they are – have nothing to do with the facts of the matter, but simply point out your very low view of God Himself.

With respect to those who believe the Bible is *untrustworthy*, that belief is really due to the fact that they simply do not accept God to be powerful enough to write a book over the space of 1,600 years using roughly 40 human authors and *still* have a book that represents His Word and His Truth. That's on the person, not God. God is able, in spite of a person's low opinion of Him and regardless of how they would like to couch their argument "intellectually."

But let's get back to the play because intermission is almost over. The production in question takes narratives from the Bible and gives them a decidedly "hilarious," "satirical" look, but probably the worst part of the play is the fact that it was produced in part with *taxpayer* dollars. There are numerous video clips from the rehearsal of the production.[50]

There are also numerous photos of the people who gathered to protest the play, and judging by that it appears as though folks are fed up with political correctness, and it's about time. There were plenty of silent protests by good people who are tired – *very* tired – of their beliefs being either taken for granted or vilified. The message they had for those who believe it is not only fine but acceptable to attack a Christian's beliefs is that it needs to stop.

Those within the politically correct crowd believe that hate speech should be against the law when it comes to *their* personal beliefs or lifestyle – when they are on the receiving end of it – and of course they define what hate speech is for *them*. Yet it is fine when they use hate speech (in the form of a satire, in this case) to direct their ire and hatred toward Christians and Jesus. The hypocrisy is blatant.

There were small groups of gays and lesbians on hand to support the play as well. Certainly, they have that right; as much right as those who are against the play. By the way, the one good thing about this situation is that there were no reported instances of violence.

However, the animosity toward those assembled to protest the play was evident. *"However, their hate for religion, the Bible, and Christianity in particular was unmistakable. And despite the muted nature of their counter-protest, a few could not hold back. 'They were there to stick a finger in our eyes,' Mike Franco told us, and a few came and got in people's faces. He said that one of them approached a pro-family man with a cap on and berated him for being a 'hypocrite' if the cap had two kinds of materials in it -- an ignorant reference to passages in*

---

[50] http://www.youtube.com/watch?feature=player_embedded&v=0kJck3pTupA (03/26/2013)

*Leviticus and Deuteronomy often quoted by homosexual activists.*"⁵¹ These types of folks always fail to understand the difference between God's moral code, which applies to all people, and aspects of the Mosaic Law, which only applied to Israel.

Romans 1:18-19 tells us, *"For the wrath of God is revealed from heaven against all ungodliness and unrighteousness of men who suppress the truth in unrighteousness, because that which is known about God is evident within them; for God made it evident to them."*

Here, Paul informs us that the truth about God is *evident*. Why? It is because God has *made* it evident. People resent Christians, Christianity, and the Bible because of the constant reminders of the fact that God has made His truth *clear*. They want this truth obliterated from society as a whole.

The next few verses are also very telling. *"For since the creation of the world His invisible attributes, His eternal power and divine nature, have been clearly seen, being understood through what has been made, so that they are without excuse. For even though they knew God, they did not honor Him as God or give thanks, but they became futile in their speculations, and their foolish heart was darkened"* (Romans 1:20-21).

Paul affirms that God's attributes are "clearly seen." How? In the very creation of the world. People will not be able to stand before God and say, *"But Lord, I had no idea you really created everything. No one told me."* He told them, through *Creation*.

So Paul *then* tells us that people go from rejecting the clear truth about God, to choosing *not* to acknowledge Him, to then choosing to *dishonor* Him, to finally becoming *futile* in the speculations. What a terrible downward spiral we see here. The result is that *"their foolish*

---

⁵¹ http://www.massresistance.org/docs/gen2/13a/PVPA-play-031513/protest.html (03/22/2013)

*heart was darkened."* They are fools because they reject what is plainly *obvious*. Their minds become darkened because of that rejection of truth. Simple, but sad. They eventually arrive to the point where they cannot see the light of truth at all because their hearts are so darkened by *lies* they have willfully embraced; yet tragically they still see themselves as intelligent, certainly more intelligent than those who believe in the antiquated narrative of Scripture.

At this point, people have actually become something they were never meant to be: *intellectual zombies*. Notice the way it works. People are born into this world and God has provided signs all over His Creation that point to Him. The signs are very obvious, which many choose to reject. It makes them angry that they are constantly reminded of the fact that God is Creator and that He has moral absolutes. They pursue their own belief that God does *not* exist, that the Bible was written by humans *only*, that it has no real truth in it, that Jesus either did not live at all or was not who He was made out to be, and so on.

After years of pursuing this, God finally *throws* them over to themselves. *"Therefore God gave them over in the lusts of their hearts to impurity, so that their bodies would be dishonored among them. For they exchanged the truth of God for a lie, and worshiped and served the creature rather than the Creator, who is blessed forever. Amen"* (Romans 1:24-25).

These people get to a point where they want so desperately to be free of even *thinking* that there is a God as described in the Bible that God finally gives them their wish. He frees them from the "tyranny" of knowing that He exists and then watches them commit spiritual suicide as they turn more inward with each passing day.

These people believe they have *arrived* and are now above the outmoded and erroneous beliefs regarding the Bible, Christianity, and

Jesus. They see true Christians as being harbingers of hate. What did Jesus say? The world hated Him and it will also hate us.

The politically correct of today believe with all their heart that they must overturn and even eradicate Christianity at all costs. There are plenty of people who call themselves Christians who, unfortunately, work side-by-side with these types of people. Why? Because they have no real understanding of what it means to actually *be* a Christian, even though Jesus took the time to explain it in John 3.

In the parable of the wheat and the tares, it is very clear that tares were sown into the farmer's fields by an enemy. The tares grew up along with the wheat, though the tares were *not* wheat. At early stages, tares look very similar to the authentic product. It can be difficult to discern the differences.

Most people in the world do not understand that there are plenty of people within Christendom who are Christian *in name only*. They go to church, they read the Bible (often taking it with a grain of salt, if that), they pray, they give money to their church, and a host of other things, but in reality, it is simply a way of life to them. Five or ten years from now, they could just as easily leave Christianity for Buddhism and still believe that "God" is with them.

I think today's authentic Christian must stand separate from the world. In part, that means being willing to stand up against the *Politically Correct Police,* as difficult as that can be at times.

Jesus stood up against the politically correct religious leaders of His day. They were politically correct charlatans who held *not* to authentic biblical teachings but to newly created traditions that they themselves instituted. The Pharisees came into existence between the testaments during a time when the Temple did not exist and the sacrificial system had been placed on hold because of it.

These Pharisees created a new system in the absence of the Mosaic sacrificial system. It was all extra-biblical and Jesus spoke against their *political correctness* at every turn. He lambasted them because they placed their *new* traditions above God's absolute truth.

Authentic Christians of today must be willing to stand against political correctness, even if in *silent* protest. If we don't do this, then how can we say we truly *love* people?

Loving people does not mean ignoring bad things in society. Truly loving people means pointing out what is wrong in society and showing the answer as well. Too many people today (Christians among them) believe that loving people means *agreeing* with them or *approving* of their choices. That's not biblical. Jesus never did that.

Truly loving people means helping others to understand what is keeping them from being in relationship with God. The people who protested the sacrilegious play in Massachusetts did so because they love God, love His truth, and desperately want others to know the same truth. Those who came to protest the protestors did so because they love *themselves* more than anything. They care not for God's truth, but only their relativism.

Romans 1 speaks to the past, but it speaks to the present and future as well. Those who continue to reject His truth will reap what they sow. True Christians need to be on the battle lines doing what we can to call attention to the lies that these precious lost people have embraced and are living. God loves them and we love them. It is *because* of that love that we are willing to show them where they are in error. Those who call themselves Christian but are not willing to do that don't love those people at all. They only love themselves and are more concerned with people thinking highly of them. They are not carrying their cross. They are more interested in the accolades of people.

Jesus was not concerned about how people thought of Him. He lived the truth and He loved people. Some received His love, but most rejected it. What about you?

# Chapter 14
# **Critical Race Theory**

In yet another example of *political correctness* taken to extremes, controversial teaching material in at least one Wisconsin school comes right out and blames white people for racism.[52] That program is called *"CREATE Wisconsin,"*[53] and like many things produced by the *politically correct* the title has absolutely nothing to do with

---

[52] http://weaselzippers.us/2013/03/19/wisconsin-teachers-taught-racism-is-caused-by-white-people/ (03/26/2013)
[53] http://weaselzippers.us/2013/03/18/wisconsin-teacher-program-focuses-on-white-privilege-creating-separate-standards-for-minority-students/ (03/26/2013)

the subject matter within the program. It is a form of subterfuge that the Left has gotten down to a science.

There is a twenty minute video from the *EAG Foundation* highlighting what they believe are the problems within the program at Delavan-Darien High School in Delavan, WI. [54] One individual noted after watching the video, "*Cultural Marxism at its finest. Another reason to put your kids in private schools.*"

All of this is based on what is known as *critical race theory,* which gained notoriety in the mid-1980s. "*In critical race* **theory***, white privilege is a set of advantages that are* **believed** *to be enjoyed by white people beyond those commonly experienced by non-white people in the same social, political, and economic spaces (nation, community, workplace, income, etc.).*

"*Theorists* **differentiate it from racism or prejudice** *because, they say, a person who may benefit from white privilege is not necessarily racist or prejudiced and* **may be unaware of having any privileges reserved only for whites**."[55] [emphasis added]

Should it be surprising that the main people promoting critical race theory are individuals who are *black*?[56] Or is that too far removed from the *politically correct arena* to even allow the question?

So, the white person who allegedly enjoys the benefits of so-called *white privilege* can do so without even *realizing* it? This is a subtle statement to suggest that *because* a person is *white* (and for no other reason), jobs come their way, friends come their way, money comes

---

[54] http://www.youtube.com/watch?feature=player_embedded&v=lmDTbWkt9ks (03/26.2013)
[55] http://en.wikipedia.org/wiki/Critical_race_theory (03/26/2013)
[56] http://www.huffingtonpost.com/2013/01/16/white-privilege-class-at-_n_2489997.html (03/26/2013)

their way, and in short, all manner of opportunities come their way which generally do *not* come to non-whites in similar situations.

If we seriously look at this issue, it should become clear that the only white people who should be actually included in the "white privilege" category are those who are very wealthy and therefore have *power*. The rest of us white folks have no special privileges at all, or power. We are often at the back of the line because there are so many minorities ahead of us, having been placed their arbitrarily due to their ethnicity. The belief that because a person is white they are automatically in the position to receive untold benefits over and above others is not true, yet it is the type of cultural Marxism that has gained a footing in America, due solely to *political correctness*.

In essence, *critical race theory* artificially *props* up one person while *undermining* another person's value solely based on the color of their skin. Since it is *believed* that white people are somehow automatically *privileged* by virtue of the color of their skin (as well as *the* cause of racism), whites are then normally kept out of the process that other races *enjoy* because of race.

What is by far the worst part of this is that it is nothing more than a *theory* propagated largely by *minorities* against *whites*, with no real proof used to buttress that theory whatsoever. It is a sweeping generalization that is not only *untrue*, but due to its negative connotations, it is *racist* to the core. How can the theory even be *proven*?

But notice how the above definition goes further, essentially claiming that a white person *is* often the *recipient* of white privilege without even realizing it. So, as one example, I'm to believe that any job I have ever gotten was due to being white, not because I may have been qualified. Any minorities who may have applied for that same job were not offered it because of "white privilege." Apparently, proof is not needed to establish a program like "*CREATE Wisconsin.*" If it simply *sounds* plausible, that's good enough.

We have the NAACP, Black Caucus, the Hispanic Caucus, the Woman's Caucus, other groups that specifically exist to help minorities with jobs and business startups, and a plethora of additional groups that work to defend the rights of *minorities*. This often takes place at the *expense* of rights for whites, justified on the basis of "white privilege," which again is nothing more than a *theory* put forth by mainly black individuals and has the trappings of racism.

Years ago, especially within Europe, white families held the reigns with all or most of the power because they had a good portion of the money. Yet there were plenty of other white families who had nothing, who worked like dogs, and in many cases were little more than slaves at best. They certainly did not benefit from the white families that *did* have the money and resultant power. These white people were every bit as undervalued and underappreciated as the next person or family, regardless of race.

Not long after America began, several families like the *Vanderbilts*, the *Carnegies*, the *Morgans*, the *Rockefellers*, and the *Fords* did whatever they could to gain and ensure their own wealth, regardless of what it meant for the "little" (white) guy. They created privilege for themselves through ruthless tactics employed to grow and protect their financial empires. They didn't care who they crushed, including their own (white) workers or other competitors (mainly white at the time).

That same money, power, and privilege has passed down to successive generations today. The Rockefellers *still* exist and they are among the richest in this nation and much of the world. It is the same with all of them. Because of the wealth they attracted to themselves they gained tremendous *power* and with it tremendous *privi-*

*lege*. (Research eugenics to understand how the Rockefellers worked with people like Margaret Sanger, from whom Planned Parenthood came into existence.)

The exact same thing applies today. People who have lots of money have power, and this is *not* solely a staple of some white people. Jay-Z, Beyonce, Eddie Murphy, Dave Chappelle, Chris Rock, and any number of black artists *or* other non-white artists and celebrities have amassed millions of dollars for themselves. That has allowed them to step into the *privileged* class of people where the average person (including whites) will *never* be able to go.

So the bottom line is that it is *not* race that brings a person privilege anymore. It is *money* that *buys* it and people of all races have money (and that has never been more true than today). It is the money they attract that puts them in the privileged class, *not* the color of their skin.

The program in Wisconsin notes and asks students, "*(R)acism is caused by white people, by our attitudes, behaviors, practices, and institutions ... How do you justify it for yourself?*"[57] In one fell swoop, all racism is laid at the feet of the white race, without proof. The very statement removes people of color from any connection to racism. It negates the idea that people of color can be racist themselves and even if this is grudgingly admitted, the fault still clearly lies with the white race. Allegedly, had not white people been racist, racism would not exist in the world. That is the unmitigated implication.

Yet there have been all sorts of racist ideas and attitudes as well as ethnic *cleansings* in many parts of the world that have nothing to do with white people lording it over minorities. In Ireland, Protestants

---

[57] http://weaselzippers.us/2013/03/19/wisconsin-teachers-taught-racism-is-caused-by-white-people/ (03/26/2013)

and Catholics hate each other and most are white. (What a great example of Christianity in action, isn't it?)

In the former Yugoslavia, Serbs and Croats killed each other because of hatred, not the color of their skin. Racial or ethnic hatred is not necessarily dependent on skin color as many within the politically correct arena of the Left in this country want us to believe.

When I taught in the public schools of California, I was disgusted to learn that Hmong and Laotian people hated each other. The Hmong were "farmers" and "hill people" while the Lao lived in towns and cities. Therefore, the Lao were far more educated and "civilized" than the Hmong. The area of California where I lived had large numbers of *both* groups and you can imagine the tension that existed between them. Young people from both cultures formed street gangs against the other culture. They brought their hatred of one another to America. It had nothing to do with white people.

Throughout history, many ethnic groups joined together to fight other ethnic groups and it was all based on race and some twisted sense of "privilege" that one race allegedly had or exercised over another. Whites are not the sole proprietors of racism. *All* races have racists within them. Racism itself is a result of the fall of humanity and *that* is a result of a failure to believe what God has said is *truth*.

Yet we have politically correct Leftists doing their level best to foment class and racial division within society. They first want to lay the blame for racism at the feet of the white race, and second, they want the guilt they hope to create within the white person to cause them to *willingly* take a seat in the back of the bus. In other words, these politically correct Leftists will not be happy until whites are on the constant receiving end of racism while blaming themselves for it at the same time.

However, the *real progenitors* of "white privilege," the Rockefellers, et al, stand in the background heartily laughing at what their privileged status has allowed them to create in society while remaining aloof from it. Their misuse of power is not the fault of whites in general, and whites, *as a race*, should not be blamed for it or held in contempt simply because the color of our skin happens to match theirs.

How does a program like the one taught at Delavan-Darien High School engender equality or a true understanding of the situation? It doesn't, because it is *not* designed to do that. It attempts to create lies, along with more stereotypes and negative behavior against whites, stoking the fires of alleged "privilege." Nothing good can come of this because it is based on a lie. Instead, guilt and shame that white students and teachers are supposed to feel for their "privileged" status will be the (hoped-for) result.

It does not cease to amaze me how low the politically correct will stoop in order to bring about *their* desired end. What they want is not only class warfare (i.e. Occupy Movement) but racial division *and* warfare as well.

The "experts" will ballyhoo and rally around "*CREATE Wisconsin*" as the next best thing within the educational morass. If we could eliminate all the extra garbage that my colleagues and I had to teach, teachers might actually be able to focus on information that would provide every student with the basics that will give him or her a leg up on life: *reading, writing, and math*.

Instead, schools have become bureaus of indoctrination where the norm includes a continued glorification of acrimony, upheaval and social distress. Young people need to stop being the emotional and mental experiment of *Cultural Marxists* whose real agenda is nothing less than a complete mental makeover to ready them for the coming one-world government.

If this was the type of situation our own children faced when they attended public school, they would have been homeschooled instead of placed in an environment where the "state" has its constant sway over them.  Parents really need to take heed and know what is being taught in their student's classrooms.

# Chapter 15
# Sound Political Theology

In a very real sense, conservatism – whether biblical or political – is under fire today because it is said that a belief system based on conservative *ideas* often serves to benefit only one group: *heterosexual, able-bodied Christians (mainly male at that)*. That belief is faulty at best, but that does not stop those opposed to conservative values from continuing the attack.

On many fronts, the notion that conservatism can be or is a good thing is highly debated by many (especially from the politically correct Left), enough so that there is a felt need to continue to malign and castigate those within the community of conservatives. Ultimately, the feeling is that it should be overturned and replaced with something else entirely since it is also believed that conservatism falls woefully short of creating true equality and freedom within society.

Of course, what people say and believe is one thing. What they can prove is another altogether, and we saw shades of this with our last chapter on Critical Race Theory. Truth really does not seem to matter to the politically correct. The only thing that matters is if it sounds like it could be true and whether or not it fits their unspoken agenda.

I was reading an article by Dr. Michael Bauman called "Begin Here: Civility or Equality?"[58] It struck a nerve, largely because the things he discusses resonate within me as I see how they impact society. Obviously, the idea of a "civilization" is based on people being civil to one another. His thesis statement is that sound political theology is the best way to bring that about throughout all of society.

But of course, what we have throughout society today is anything but sound political theology, in my opinion. It is more like open season on anything that even smacks of true conservatism because conservatism should be disallowed.

The rhetoric from those opposed to conservatism is heated, often libelous, and too often absurd, though they refuse to see it that way or admit to it, even when it is clear they are making statements that are patently false and even irrelevant. Yet the vehemence with which they address the issue of conservatism is done to polarize those who firmly believe that conservatism best represents the actual biblical revelation from God as well as the attendant mandate for society.

---

[58] http://www.theimaginativeconservative.org/begin-here-civility-equality/#.UUneXVd5ckV (03/26/2013)

Bauman notes several things about what he refers to as sound political theology. *"Sound political theology is the means by which we can identify the insights of revelation and apply them prudently to the political order. Sound political theology is the wisdom and moral imagination that springs from revelation properly understood and wisely applied. Sound political theology is the theologically and historically informed prudence necessary to preserve the best of the past for ourselves and for our posterity in light of what God has done and said. Sadly, even tragically, political theology of this high order is as rare as it is necessary."*[59]

In truth, sound political theology as referenced by Bauman is fast becoming outmoded, pushed to the side by the politically correct militants of our day, who desperately feel the need to throw off the fetters that remind us of God's authority over His Creation. The desire of today is to replace, redefine, and renege. But like many things emanating from the politically correct arena, the premise of many within those groups that purpose to accomplish this is flawed at best.

That premise starts with something that has nothing to do with God's absolute truth and everything to do with a thorny relativism that impinges and contorts reality into something that is not discernible, yet claims to be the actual and informed meaning of God's truth. In short, it sets out to produce what by God's standards is a very poor shadow of His absolute truth – a very poor shadow indeed. Yet in reality, this is the best that Satan can come up with. What could possibly be better than God's absolutes for a people or a nation, or for the world and all of God's Creation, for that matter?

Bauman speaks of the fact that many in society chase after and even demand equality and freedom when they should instead be pursuing justice since both equality and freedom are to him antithetical. The

---

[59] http://www.theimaginativeconservative.org/begin-here-civility-equality/#.UUneXVd5ckV (03/26/2013)

more we pursue equality and/or freedom, the less justice there is in the world, because for each person, there is a new definition of freedom...for them. This ever-changing definition of freedom creates injustice for someone else. When someone desires more freedom, as Bauman notes, the first rational question to ask is, freedom to do what? There is no definitive notion of freedom that works for everyone. It is not a one-size fits all commodity.

Therefore, he notes further that *"unlike equality and freedom, justice is not an impracticable metaphysical abstraction. Justice is getting what you deserve. The pursuit and preservation of justice maintains the order of soul and of society necessary for human flourishing.*

*"To the requirements of justice, we all are born subject. No contrivance, political or otherwise, can or should extricate us from its obligations, which come from God Himself. To reject these obligations is to tear apart the fabric both of soul and of society. No person, no polity, can long endure, much less prosper, outside the obligations of justice."*[60]

When contemplated, the facts inherent within the above statements speak for themselves. Unfortunately, the opposite is what is happening within society today because of the dereliction of duty by our elected officials (who have sworn to uphold the rule of law of America, but fail to follow through on that promise) as well as the fallacies instilled in America from those within the politically correct arena that are given too much sway in society.

We cannot at the same time allow those opposed to God's morality and absolute truth to hold their position of power in society while believing that their understanding of truth is as good as any, since it is clear that they reject God's absolutes in favor of their own thorny

---

[60] http://www.theimaginativeconservative.org/begin-here-civility-equality/#.UUneXVd5ckV (03/26/2013)

relativism. These forces are at odds and there is no way to marry them. The choice then becomes: which one to follow?

Bauman speaks of the metaphysical aspects of "equality" and "freedom" and how emphasis on these areas confuses the difference between the absolutes of God's revelation with what he calls the "sloganeering" of those opposed to them. Of course, the politically correct love to create slogans and labels that they can quickly attach to anyone who opposes them. This is done to shut down dialogue and debate because those within politically correct circles cannot muster the strength or intellect to adequately respond to the facts of the matter. It is far easier and more beneficial that they do what they can to immediately squelch discussion. For them, "sloganeering" is one of the primary ways for this to be accomplished.

Imagine attempting to discuss your concerns with one of the keynote speakers from our last chapter dealing with "*CREATE sin.*" Imagine how quickly you would be called a racist (or something else, depending upon your race) if you dared question the motives, the rationale, or the facts surrounding what these individuals believe and propose regarding critical race theory.

If you watched the video we mentioned in the last chapter[61], you saw how the Superintendent of Public School Instruction of Wisconsin was really unable to answer the question posed by the interviewer. He did what he could to misdirect and foist blame back on the individual asking the question. This is the game as far as they are concerned. It has to do with kowtowing to a group, whether or not facts support the direction that group is moving in. Because of political correctness, ideas are often deemed correct in spite of the lack of factual support for those ideas, especially when it has to do with things like "white privilege."

---

[61] http://www.youtube.com/watch?feature=player_embedded&v=lmDTbWkt9ks

Bauman notes, *"In short, we must not begin with metaphysical abstractions, no matter how desirable we might think they are. We begin with revelation and with the world as it is in all its incalculable complexity, **a complexity that mocks the facile imposition of abstractions and easy recourse to metaphysical sloganeering**. Sloganeers are fools, as are those who vote for them. Justice, for those requiring a reminder, is not an abstraction but a moral, social, and judicial obligation placed upon us by God. As much as we can do so, **we are obligated to give folks what they deserve**."*[62] [emphasis added]

I have met too many "sloganeers," and I'm sure you have as well. They believe for all their pontificating, labeling, huffing and puffing that they make great strides in society, helping to push civilization to the next higher level. Unfortunately, they do nothing of the kind, but in fact simply help the downward spiral within culture to advance that much more quickly.

Surely, Bauman's clarity here is unmistakable, even to the most intellectually disingenuous. Truth begins with God's revelation as it applies to the complexity of this world. To address the world from any other vantage point simply reduces things to perceived quick fixes that wind up not only not fixing, but making things far worse. The world is very complex, but God has the answers for that complexity and the answers are not found in the easy recourse so often focused on by politicians and the politically correct of this world.

It is like Harry Reid blaming the recent explosion and resultant deaths of the Marines on sequestration, when in point of fact the two are not related, except in his twisted mind. Yet when Reid stands up to announce the two are related, the politically correct jump on that bandwagon in agreement. Why? Because their mandate comes not from God's absolute truth. This would cause them to see the fallacy

---

[62] http://www.theimaginativeconservative.org/begin-here-civility-equality/#.UUneXVd5ckV (03/26/2013)

of their position. It comes from the meandering and pointlessness of satanically-inspired *relativism*.

In essence, righteousness – or the desire to do right by seeking and imposing true justice on the citizens of any given culture – is what solidifies a civilization's reflection and representation of the truth (and that is God's truth, not ours). Apart from this and without it, that civilization has simply sunk to a point clearly defined for us by Paul in Romans 1, as we have previously discussed.

An example of a lack of true justice is seen in the Obama administration's recent approval of a program that allows Saudis to bypass normal airport security.[63] This decision is neither fair nor just, especially if we consider the fact that many of the hijackers in the original 9/11 event came from Saudi Arabia. Yet the Obama administration believes that this fact should not dissuade them from creating a special category for Saudi citizens. Politically correct "visionaries" will hail this decision as one that portrays an agenda of freedom and equality, yet in reality, it does neither.

*"Nations are defined by their righteousness, or they are destroyed by its absence. That fact is bad news for a nation that sets aside the immutable principles of God and that replaces them with a new (but not improved) brand of culturally relative ethics."*[64] The United States – as one example – has for too many decades been actively moving away from its righteousness that was tied directly to God's unbending truth. We have ourselves to blame for it.

Yet in spite of this truth, the politically correct continue to try to throw off the *"shackles"* of God's truth (cf. Psalm 2), replacing it with

---

[63] http://directorblue.blogspot.com/2013/03/white-house-approves-program-allowing.html?utm_source=twitterfeed&utm_medium=twitter (03/26/2013)
[64] http://www.theimaginativeconservative.org/begin-here-civility-equality/#.UUneXVd5ckV (03/26/2013)

the aimlessness of relative truth, which of course, is no truth at all. It is a "*truth*" that focuses on the *freedom* and *equality* of individuals but not on the *justice* for society as a whole.

I will end this chapter with a final quote from Dr. Bauman. *"Given the self-destructive foolishness of human nature, the real question we need to ask and to answer is 'How are we to spare ourselves the ravages of anarchy and evil?'*

*"The answer is revelation, solid families, prudent government, and the wisdom of the ages. Nothing else can domesticate the savage lurking just beneath our skin. The less fully we recognize that savage's existence and identity, the more control he has over us — indeed the more fully he **is** us."*[65] [emphasis in original]

---

[65] http://www.theimaginativeconservative.org/begin-here-civility-equality/#.UUneXVd5ckV (03/26/2013)

# Chapter 16
# Fort Hood's Political Correctness

In 2009, Islamic terrorist Maj. Nidal Malik Hasan, an Army psychiatrist, with malice aforethought gunned down thirteen military personnel and attempted to murder thirty-two others at Fort Hood, TX. While he was in the process of shooting indiscriminately at the military personnel gathered in the cafeteria, he was heard yelling *"Allahu Akbar!"* which means "Allah is Great!"

Shortly after the massacre, Obama came out to report to the nation that while the event was terrible, it was nothing more than "workplace violence" in spite of the alleged connections to Islam and that *"Hasan allegedly was inspired by a member of Al Qaeda in Yemen,*

*Anwar Awlaki, an American who was later killed in a U.S. drone strike.*"[66] I guess shouting praise to Allah while killing innocent people does not by itself mean that you are a terrorist. However, if you defend the Constitution and demand your rights that are given because of it, well, you just might be a terrorist, even if you never harm another person.

Since Hasan's arrest and imprisonment, there have been a number of attempts by Hasan's lawyers to draw out the proceedings, including the situation involving his beard. Army rules indicate that he must be clean-shaven during trial, yet he argues that it is against his religious beliefs (though he had been previously clean-shaven). One judge has already been replaced because he attempted to stand by the rules and ordered Hasan to be forcefully shaved. The new judge has not yet ruled on that particular question.

The tragedy – aside from the murders and attempted murders of our military people – is that Hasan is being catered to by a politically correct (corrupt?) administration and others who would like us to believe that Hasan's terrible act of cowardice has nothing to do with Islam and everything to do with a man who cracked in the workplace.

Numerous efforts to have the situation reclassified as "terrorism" have been denied by the Pentagon. Such is how the politically correct craft their lies, and because they hold the bulk of power now, they are essentially free to do what they wish to do. They are backed by the media, who share the same mindset and mission: to prop up relativistic "truth" via political correctness.

I fully believe that this world is heading toward the judgment of the coming Tribulation. I also realize that there are many who think

---

[66] http://www.jihadwatch.org/2013/03/judge-rules-against-fort-hood-jihad-mass-murderer-trial-will-stay-in-texas-and-he-cant-plead-guilty.html?utm_source=dlvr.it&utm_medium=twitter (03/26/2013)

holding to that viewpoint is ridiculous. They are entitled to their viewpoint and obviously, in this matter, time will be the vindicator.

However, it would be nice to be able to overcome the travesties that have been created by those within the politically correct arena, though in my heart, I wonder if God will allow that because so much water has passed under the bridge.

It simply appears to me (and many others) that, political correctness being what it is, the Obama administration as well as many other areas within our society are doing their level best to overturn and eliminate absolute truth with their relativism in order to tear down the values upon which this country was founded. Yes, I've said that before, but it bears repeating.

The thing that really stands out is how these politically correct charlatans can lie as they do with a straight face. Even when their lies become known as the lies that they are, they continue on that path, refusing to acknowledge that they are liars and that their entire premise is built on a lie.

A few days ago a reporter asked Jay Carney whether or not Obama was going to pull back on all of his expensive golf outings and vacations now that sequestration is in the mix. Carney's response was obviously duplicitous but presented in a way that was supposed to allow no one to question it. He essentially stated that Obama is always thinking about the situation that America faces. There is not a time when it does not occupy his mind. That's my paraphrase, but the response to that is, "So?" Thinking about something and doing something about it are two different things.

We know from a complete lack of action from the White House that Obama does not take the situation seriously. A budget won't be coming from the White House until April, yet by law, it was supposed to have been submitted by the White House in February. Bush would not have gotten away with doing what Obama is doing, but because of the amount of politically correct news bureaus, this is easy to let slide when it concerns Obama because he is in the same camp as the news bureaus.

It is for this reason that these same news bureaus are ignoring the Fort Hood situation. They are not demanding that the event be re-classified a terrorist event. They are not siding against Obama in his labeling of the event as "workplace violence."

By the same token, they are not questioning the Obama administration's decision to allow Saudi citizens to bypass the normal aspects of airport security that all Americans are subject to: this is in spite of the fact that fifteen of the nineteen original 9/11 hijackers came from Saudi Arabia. They are not questioning these things because these news bureaus are firmly ensconced within the exact same politically correct arena as are Obama and his administration. Right now, they have the power, and it is difficult to get anyone's attention. When we are able to get their attention, it is fairly easy for them to slide it back under the rug.

But tell me, why should anyone be given special status to avoid having to submit to the security requirements of the TSA at airports if they are not even citizens of this country? If anyone should be exempted, it should be our military. Certainly, a Marine should not be required to remove his prosthesis and then be forced to stand (effectively on his knees!) while some less-than-clueless (or uncaring) TSA agent swabs down his wheelchair!

This is what political correctness does. It promotes *not* justice (as we discussed in our last chapter), but some type of artificial "freedom" and "equality," yet the way it accomplishes this is not by generating equality for *all* people but by artificially creating a "greater equality" for some while ignoring others due to perceived slights for those within the elevated group.

There is no good or fair reason that the Fort Hood massacre should be considered "workplace violence" when it is *clearly* terrorism within our own borders. Timothy McVeigh was guilty of terrorism and there was no problem calling it that. Then again, he was a white male, so that alone makes it easier.

In spite of the fact that since 9/11 Islamists have carried out 20,569 attacks throughout the world, the Obama administration has deemed it important to allow Saudi citizens to bypass TSA security at US airports. Moreover, the Obama administration has also refused to classify the Fort Hood massacre as an act of terrorism, preferring the more benign "workplace violence."

Yet in all the acrimonious testimony related to the recent gun control legislation, not once did anyone from the Obama administration elect to refer to this "workplace violence" in which a gun was used to kill thirteen people and wound thirty-two more. Why? What was the problem? After all, it was only "workplace violence," wasn't it? No, it was an act of terror by an Islamic terrorist who is still receiving full pay as an Army psychiatrist.

Political correctness is a terrible thing. It creates a counterfeit reality that simply mocks the true reality. It sets up unwritten, fake rules and guidelines for castigating one race while upholding other races. It accomplishes nothing good but engenders fear and self-loathing for non-minorities while creating a special, privileged place for minorities.

It is because of political correctness that we are living in a world that Isaiah saw years ago. He said (in Isaiah 5:20), *"Woe to those who call evil good, and good evil; Who substitute darkness for light and light for darkness; Who substitute bitter for sweet and sweet for bitter!"*

In the same way Paul, in writing to Timothy, warned that in the end times, the world would become terrible. This would be so because it has been the attempt of humanity to exchange God's truth for a lie at every turn. It began in the Garden of Eden and will carry us through to the end. In 2 Timothy 3:13, Paul states, *"But evil men and impostors will proceed from bad to worse, deceiving and being deceived."*

This is what we are experiencing now. This country is being guided largely by evil men and women who want one thing: to exchange the truth of God for a lie (cf. Romans 1:25). This is best accomplished using what has become known as political correctness.

Political correctness uses terms and phrases that appear to be couched in logic and truth, but in reality, it is all simply another form of lying and presented in a way that makes it difficult for the hearer to reject without being labeled a bigot, a sexist, a racist, or all three. The goal is to quiet the opposition so that political correctness can do its work of destruction. It has been at work since the early 1900s and came to the surface during the tumultuous '60s. Since that time, it has shown tremendous gains in society until we are now at the point where it *appears* to have the minds of the majority.

Christians must resist it because it is a lie. In Paul's second letter to the Thessalonians, chapter two, he takes time to point out the events as they will unfold in the end times. He comes to a point where he essentially lays out the facts and summarizes them with this one statement: *"For this reason God will send upon them a deluding influence so that they will believe what is false"* (2 Thessalonians 2:11).

The natural question to ask is "for *what* reason" and "what is the deluding influence" Paul is referring to here? If we look at the verses just prior to verse 11, we note that the people Paul refers to here in 2 Thessalonians 2:11 do the exact same thing the people in Romans 1 do: *"They perish because they refused to love the truth and so be saved"* (2 Thessalonians 2:10b NIV).

It's the same story! People perish because they prefer lies to the truth! Throughout history, it has always been the same. *"Tell me a lie! Tell me a lie so that I don't have to believe in God or do things His way!"* It was the truth of Lot's day and of Noah's day before him. It was the situation during Jesus' day and in the final analysis, it will be the exact same thing for us during these last days.

People do *not* want God's absolute truth. They want lies because lies tickle the ears and make people feel good. The truth haunts us until we give into it. If we resolutely and consistently refuse that truth, God will eventually throw us over to ourselves and we will then be able to wholeheartedly believe the lie.

Political correctness is the lie that is guiding our society today. Its influence is everywhere. It is turning God's absolute truths on their head, endeavoring to replace them with something that the world can see and appreciate as their new truth. If they continue in this, God will throw them over to themselves so that they will believe the lie, and because of that they will perish.

Do you see how important it is for Christians to stand against political correctness? If we don't, who will? It is the Christian's stand and voice against the duplicitous nature of political correctness that keeps that falseness at bay. This is why the Christian will be increasingly hated: it is our presence that keeps the deluding influence of political correctness from doing more damage than it could be doing.

## Chapter 17
# Politically Correct Ignorance

To those who are adamantly entrenched in the politically correct Left, it is important to hide, dodge, and redirect the actions of people who are believed to be protected by political correctness. In fact, because of the cultural Marxism that is sweeping the world, including America, even criminal activity should be tolerated by *omitting* or not *reporting all the facts of* it. Never is this more clearly seen than in the growing area of incidents of *rapes*.

Throughout parts of Europe (including the UK and even into India), marauding groups of Muslims seem to have taken to the streets for the sole purpose of *raping* women. Of course, they feel they have a right to do this since the women are "uncovered" and are therefore no better than "whores," "sluts," and "prostitutes." As such, they get what they deserve, according to Islam's Sharia law. This attitude toward women is – unbelievably – ignored in many ways by the media *and* the politically correct. Muslims have been granted a type of "victimhood" status that compels the politically correct to react to them differently than they would, say, if gangs of white men roamed around Europe and perpetrated the same types of crimes against women.

The terribly unfortunate part of this (aside from the trauma of being raped) is the fact that the media is under-reporting these events across the globe. One article states, *"High profile-gang rapes in India have been in the headlines since December. The phenomenon is growing across Europe too, but tends to be under reported due to the high incidence of Muslim perpetrators which makes it politically incorrect to mention."*[67]

You may have read of some of these reports, but it's also likely that you did not read that the perpetrators were Muslim. You probably read that the men who are said to have committed these crimes were "from India" or "Sweden" or even "Asian," but nothing more. As the quote above notes, it is not politically correct to mention this glaring fact. Many officials state it has nothing to do with anything. It's better to ignore it and simply focus on the fact that the perpetrators are men.

But what if a group's ideology believes and even allows for men within that group to treat women in such a horrific way in order to send a message: cover up or be raped as punishment? Of course, to the politically correct that statement is offensive because it smacks of bigotry. However, this belief appears to have some basis for why many

---

[67] http://creepingsharia.wordpress.com/2013/03/21/muslim-gang-rapes-across-europe-under-reported-in-press/ (03/26/2013)

Muslim men (and young boys) act as they do toward women who are uncovered. Is it another form of Islamic jihad that is attempting to force women to cover themselves up by making it so difficult for them to even walk down the street without fear of being verbally assaulted, at the very least? If this is the case, then should officials and good people everywhere be concerned? What is the answer, to force women to wear burkas in order to avoid being raped? If so, then might it be that in the end, we give these Muslims what they want and Sharia has won...again?

In reality, as far as the politically correct are concerned, the only time it is beneficial or "right" to mention a person's ethnicity or religious heritage is when they are being honored for something. So, when my local paper highlights a group of "African-American" Sci-Fi writers, that's perfectly fine. It is within the boundaries of political correctness to do that. However, since most Muslims are Arab (though anyone can be a Muslim since it is not dependent upon race or ethnicity), they fall in that group we call "minorities" even if/when they are not truly minorities numerically.

In one rape case in India, the poor woman was traumatized for seven (7) hours while up to twelve Afghan immigrants took turns raping her repeatedly. This went on while the men also called her "slut" and "whore" and then clapped and cheered during the attack. The woman is now confined to a wheelchair (due to her injuries), has panic attacks, and resides in a psychiatric hospital.

If this was a unique situation, it would be bad enough. However, incidents of this type are fast becoming the norm throughout Europe. The article from which I've quoted also discusses how the UK reports these situations. Interestingly enough, in the UK press these perpetrators are most often referred to as "Asian" even though they are Muslim. As the article points out, *"The Asian gangs do not contain rapists from China, Japan, and the Philippines."*[68]

In other words, "Asian" appears to be code for "Muslim" as used by the media in the UK. If I were an actual Asian individual, I would be pretty upset that I (and others like me) was being blamed for something I had no part in.

There are many young girls in the UK who are either raped or groomed for prostitution by these "Asians." *"According to some of the mothers, a fear of being branded racist makes many of the police and social services reluctant to investigate the crimes as organised (sic) and connected. One mother from Rotherham, whose 14-year-old daughter was groomed into prostitution and multiply raped during a 12-month period, told me that almost every man convicted of these crimes in the north of England is from Pakistan but that the authorities insist that it is not relevant."*[69]

Of *course* it's relevant that they are from Pakistan! Political correctness says it's not relevant, but that's only because political correctness cares not for justice at all, as we have already determined previously. There are alarming statistics of the increase in violent rapes by Muslims against non-Muslim girls and women. It has led many to question why there is this deafening silence regarding the fact that, by far, the majority of perpetrators are Muslim.

After describing a particularly terrible situation in which two young girls of France were kidnapped, held over a two-year period, and raped by up to twenty-five men daily (all of whom turned out to be Muslim), one article stated, *"The thing is... the convicted men are all Muslims. At least, they have recognisably (sic) Islamic names. Yet the mainstream press are not reporting this fact. Is this religio-cultural as-*

---

[68] http://creepingsharia.wordpress.com/2013/03/21/muslim-gang-rapes-across-europe-under-reported-in-press/ (03/26/2013)
[69] Ibid

*pect of French gang culture taboo? As much as it appears to be in the UK? Why the whitewash? Why the ethno-religious censorship? Why is the issue of gang-rape committed by young men identified as belonging to a particular minority background consistently suppressed? Are there reporting restrictions? Infringement of their human rights? A conspiracy of silence?"*[70]

Of course, with the influx of Muslims into America, we are starting to see this type of "take what I want" mentality here as well. In just one case, a Virginia woman alleges she was raped by the taxi driver who took her home.[71] What is interesting here is that the woman went to the hospital and very likely had a DNA swab done. The man stated that the woman tried to seduce him but he ignored her. The man's wife (who does not live in Virginia) stated that the woman was lying, that her husband would never have tried to rape a woman.

Ultimately though, the US Attorney has opted to not pursue charges against the cabbie. Why? There is no reason given, except the politically correct statement that "the investigation is ongoing," designed to make us think that something is still being done and considered, when in point of fact, that is likely not the case.

We know that Muslim men from Europe and the Middle East believe that a woman who is uncovered (without burka or face covering) is no better than a prostitute. Sweden has been experiencing the problem of growing numbers of rapes and attempted rapes for a few years. Women there report the constant harassment by Muslims who call them all sorts of despicable names simply because they walk around without a burka. Many Islamic Imams blame the woman for the man's arousal. For this reason, women should be covered so that

---

[70] http://archbishop-cranmer.blogspot.gr/2012/10/muslim-gang-rape-in-france.html (03/26/2013)
[71] http://creepingsharia.wordpress.com/2013/03/21/u-s-attorney-not-pursuing-charges-against-muslim-cabbie-accused-of-rape/ (03/26/2013)

the temptation is avoided by men. The responsibility rests with the woman.

So when they come to America (or some other country) where women dress in skirts, dresses, or wear shorts and tank tops, these men harbor the same low view of women that they held in their former country. In those countries, they were used to seeing women covered up, and a woman who was uncovered was essentially "asking for it." If she was raped, it was her own fault.

Even though men are often arrested for the rapes they commit, political correctness disallows the world to point to the man's religious beliefs as the reason he believes he can rape a woman. The fact that no one is doing anything to help these men change their view regarding women allows it to continue.

Some would argue that being arrested should get the message across. In too many cases, it does not. They are arrested, go to jail, come out and rape some more. Going to jail is a minor problem for them.

In another example of political correctness and its desire to eradicate all semblance of Christianity and biblical values from American society, one Florida University student complained that during his intercultural communications class, the professor allegedly *"told the whole class to write the name JESUS in bold letters on a piece of paper, then drop the papers and stomp all over them."*[72]

The student said that some students did what the professor told them to do, while he and several other students did not participate. After class, he told the professor, Deandre Poole, that what he asked the class to do offended his religious convictions (the student

---

[72] http://patriotupdate.com/2013/03/florida-university-student-suspended-for-not-stomping-on-jesus/?utm_source=twitterfeed&utm_medium=twitter (03/26/2013)

is a Mormon). Hey, I wonder if the instructor buys into critical race theory.

The student eventually complained about the situation to a university official and was promptly suspended from the class.[73] So, the politically correct minions believe it is perfectly okay to stomp on the Name of Jesus. Apparently, there is some point to that. The only point I am aware of is that it is simply part of the politically correct agenda to eradicate anything that smacks of biblical values.

*"An FAU official defended the decision, telling WPEC that the Jesus-stomping was part of a classroom exercise from a textbook."*[74]

I should simply allow that statement to stand as it is, in all its asinine glory, but some might miss the point. So, if the textbook said that students should write the name of, say, Martin Luther King, Jr. on a piece of paper, drop it on the floor, and stomp on it, would that be acceptable? How about if instead of the Name Jesus, the name of Muhammad was used and stomped on? Would that be acceptable too? We all know the answer to that one.

It has to be connected to the American patriarchal system that is believed to have elevated white men above society while holding back those who come to believe that they are victims of white male prejudice. This is why Muhammad is not bothered with and Muslims are not called out for their sexism and thoroughly antiquated beliefs about women and those outside of Islam.

The focus needs to remain on Christianity and the American (white) male. I realize what I've just said it *not* politically correct. Good. While some choose to read that and believe me to be a racist, it's only because they are too afraid to think for themselves and prefer, at all

---

[73] http://dailycaller.com/2013/03/21/florida-atlantic-univ-student-claims-he-was-suspended-for-not-stomping-on-jesus-video/ (03/26/2013)
[74] Ibid

costs, to align themselves with the deluding influence of political correctness, which, in the end, only leads to cultural Marxism.

Political correctness has nothing good in it at all. Through it, cultural Marxism is meant to rule the day as it creeps consistently throughout society, remaking it into something it was never meant to be. People like Deandre Poole are helping to make that happen.

But I'd like to end this chapter on a good note. You might be interested to know that Twinkies are back! Even though Hostess was put out of business by the unbearable and unfair demands of unionized labor, another company has bought the rights to produce one of America's favorite sweet treats. At least there's one good thing on the close horizon coming our way.[75]

---

[75] http://www.freeenterprise.com/intellectual-property/hostess-mostess-twinkies-are-back (03/26/2013)

# Chapter 18
# Racial Problems in the Big City

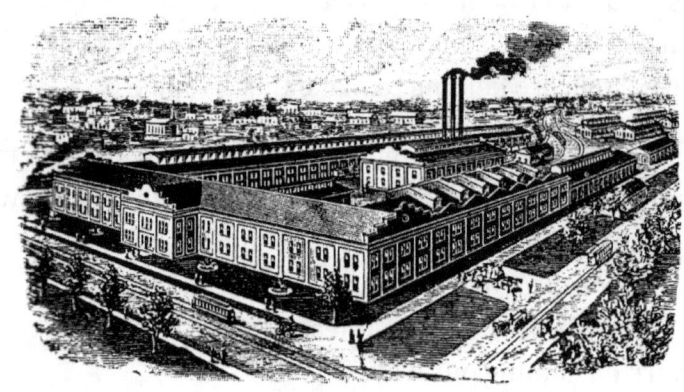

Y ou know, I used to wonder what I would do if I ran out of ideas to write about and comment on. What would I say if *that* ever happened?

However, having realized just how pervasive political correctness is throughout society (as well as understanding that the ultimate goal of political correctness via cultural Marxism is to overturn any and all semblance of the biblical and traditional values), I have realized I will likely *never* run out of things to write about. In fact, this could easily be a full-time job, focusing on and highlighting all the things in society that the politically correct cultural Marxists of our day have endeavored to actualize.

There are too many things happening that are either tinged with or completely undergirded by political correctness and with the blinders off, it has become extremely easy to recognize them and point them out. Those who profit from political correctness (financially, socially, or both) must at all costs *continue* to instigate change based on the lies, innuendo, and faulty conclusions they've drawn so that the needed societal metamorphosis continues to occur. At the very least, a state of flux, uncertainty, and insecurity within society needs to be maintained to keep people on edge and off kilter.

Realizing what is at stake allows a person to stand apart from and remain free of the ravages of political correctness, to not be affected by it, to isolate it, and even call attention to it as the true *source* of the problem. Those within the politically correct arena want to *hide* that method being used so that only the intended *results* are realized, whether those results are good for everyone or not. In truth, they are decidedly *not* good for everyone, as we have already seen in a variety of situations facing the world today. Political correctness leading to cultural Marxism only seeks to bring "equality" and "freedom" to certain groups in society, not all.

Under the PC-umbrella, certain groups are ignored and even vilified as the reason why the *other* groups must be given special status and privilege. It is all designed to allegedly even things out. But of course, the question is, when are things evened out *enough*? The short answer is, *never*.

This unwritten code that directs society causes people to go along with the agenda because people are deathly afraid of being called "racist" or "sexist" or "bigoted." No one likes that at all, especially a person who is innocent of those charges. To prove it, they will go along with the system, often without realizing it because of the pressure placed on them from others within society. This is what they do to avoid being a cast off of society as a pariah or anathema.

Referring again to what Anthony Browne has stated about how the average person makes decisions in society today, it is clear that many to most feel an obligation to come not necessarily to the *correct* answer, but to the *politically correct* one. *"For the modern mind, confronted with a new set of policy options on a difficult issue, the first reaction is not to try and divine the right answer, but the 'politically-correct' one. Many people will think first of what the true answer is, and in an effort to avoid controversy or offense, measure it up against the dictates of political correctness. Those whose intellectual faculties have been all but closed down by political correctness have learnt (sic) to automatically short-cut to the PC response."*[76]

One simple example is when black individuals would say things like *"This country will never elect a black man as president"* before the 2008 election. It assumes several things which are not true and it is actually a racist statement since it assumes that most (or all) white people are racist and would simply not vote for a black person under any condition because of the color of his skin.

It is a form of racial triple-dog-dare-ya and obviously many white people took it to heart and felt an obligation to prove what they were not. In some cases at least, white people voted for Mr. Obama for no other reason than to prove they were *not* racist. *"There, I voted for Obama. See? I'm not racist."* An asinine reason to vote for someone to be sure, yet it was done that way. This is certainly not to suggest that all white people who voted for Mr. Obama were only doing so to prove they were not racists, but it appeared as though many took the bait.

---

[76] Anthony Browne, *The Retreat of Reason* (2006), p. 5

Being white in a society that has increasingly grown hostile to white people is something that most prefer not to discuss. It *is* a real problem though, not an imaginary one. It exists because of created unproven theories that are propagated by racists from minority communities who speak in intellectually educational terms and have the letters "PhD" after their names.

Their *stated* goal is to ensure that all students of color have their place at the table and are not lost in the shuffle. This is certainly a worthwhile and necessary goal to have and pursue. However, the *unstated* goal is far different. The *unstated* goal is the evolution of minorities that will cause them to stand in line *ahead* of white people since it is long believed that whites are privileged because of their race. See my previous articles on "Critical Race Theory"[77] and "Sound Political Theology."[78]

But let's look at a few examples from an article titled "Being White in Philly" by Robert Huber. In it, he discusses issues of race and problems associated with it. He tells how his son went to Temple University and lived in a section of Philly not far from campus. Not far from his son's apartment were row houses that were not in the greatest of shape. Windows were broken, doors chained (with padlocks), and other things generally testified of the crime, tragedy, and broken humanity that lived there.

Huber notes that he'd *"begun to think that most white people stopped looking around at large segments of our city, at our poorest and most dangerous neighborhoods, a long time ago. One of the reasons, plainly put, is queasiness over race. Many of those neighborhoods are predom-*

---

[77] http://studygrowknowblog.com/2013/03/20/critical-race-theory-blaming-whites-for-racism-in-wisconsin/ (03/26/2013)
[78] http://studygrowknowblog.com/2013/03/21/can-sound-political-theology-produce-civility/ (03/26/2013)

inantly African-American. And if you're white, you don't merely avoid them—you do your best to erase them from your thoughts."[79]

Of course, that quote contains verbiage that on the surface is not considered by all to be politically correct. Yet Huber is being est. There is truth in what he has stated. He is referring to the fact that it *appears* on the surface that many within the white community do not want to consider the difficulties associated with interracial communication, so it is avoided, while giving it lip service. In truth, I'm not sure we know what to do about it, though I'm fairly certain I know what is not helping and making it worse.

He goes onto say, *"At the same time, white Philadelphians think a great deal about race. Begin to talk to people, and it's clear it's a dominant motif in and around our city. Everyone seems to have a story, often an uncomfortable story, about how white and black people relate."*[80]

It is clear from the illustrations he goes on to provide that there are plenty of examples of situations in which it is clearly difficult for whites and blacks (in this case) to come together to think the same thoughts or recognize the same motives. In one example, he speaks of a young white woman who misplaced her Blackberry. She did not know what else to do except send a message via a social network site to everyone she could think of in her class, asking if any of them had come across it.

The one black student in the class took umbrage at the post, responding with, *"Why would I just happen to pick up a BlackBerry and if this is a personal message I'm offended!"*[81] The young white woman then had to explain that she had emailed everyone at the same time (not just the black student). The black student then rejoined with *"Next*

---

[79] http://www.phillymag.com/articles/white-philly/ (03/26/2013)
[80] Ibid
[81] Ibid

*time be careful what type of messages you send around and what you say in them."*[82] There was nothing wrong with the way the young woman had approached the subject and some would say there was nothing wrong in the way the black student had responded, apart from some sensitivity.

But where does this *ultra-sensitivity* come from and how is it engendered? In spite of the tension, the woman who had lost her phone (Susan) made a concerted effort to say "hi" to the black student whenever their paths crossed (after the event) and eventually the tension evaporated. Huber points out that it was very possible that the black student – they were attending Villanova (or Vanilla-Nova, as some jokingly refer to it) – was reacting from the *"perceived lack of welcome to African-Americans [at the school]."*[83]

Huber highlights other situations and examples that speak to the *perception* of racism (whether real or imagined) that exists today. The problem is that political correctness does *nothing* to calm racial tensions or even denounce all forms of racism regardless of the person's race, but too often creates a true *oversensitivity* toward the issue. In essence, the favoritism shown to some *because* of political correctness is simply another form of racism directed toward whites, since they are the perceived creators of racism.

Robert Huber comes to much the same conclusion. He states, *"On one level, such self-consciousness and hypersensitivity can be seen as progress when it comes to race, a sign of how much attitudes have shifted for the better, a symbol of our desire for things to be better. And yet, lately I've come to fear that the opposite might also be true: that **our carefulness is, in fact, at the heart of the problem**."*[84] [emphasis added]

---

[82] http://www.phillymag.com/articles/white-philly/ (03/26/2013)
[83] Ibid
[84] Ibid

If we *have* become hypersensitive, as Huber suggests (and I would concur), this would account for the unwillingness of minorities to discuss the problem of race as it applies to whites. *"What gets examined publicly about race is generally one-dimensional, looked at almost exclusively from the perspective of people of color. Of course, it is black people who have faced generations of discrimination and who deal with it still. But our public discourse ignores the fact that race—particularly in a place like Philadelphia—is also an issue for white people. Though white people never talk about it."*[85]

Minorities do not want to hear about the potential sufferings of whites (due to political correctness or "reverse discrimination") because most don't believe whites *have* suffered or *do* suffer any form of racism. They likely believe whites *created* it, therefore whites are the guilty party: the problem.

To this we can only wonder what positive effects cultural Marxism has for society as a whole. I cannot see any at all. What I see is a society becoming far worse because of what the vehicle of political correctness has worked to define and create.

Political correctness divides, separates, and conquers. It forces people to focus on inequities, but in a way that generates *more* inequities than it can ever fix. In fact, it is not the goal of political correctness (or cultural Marxism, for that matter) to design a society in which all are equal, on the same footing. The only thing political correctness can do is try to right wrongs by establishing *new* wrongs as a way of balancing out the inequities. These are mainly directed at a group that is believed to be the primary perpetrator of all previous wrongs.

---

[85] http://www.phillymag.com/articles/white-philly/ (03/26/2013)

# Chapter 19
# Does the End Justify the Means?

**P**olitical correctness is a fascinating subject if for no other reason than the fact that an entire society of people can fall prey to the warped, restrictive, racist, guilt-creating, ad hominem-based, and overwhelmingly antithetical ideology of it.  They do so all because they allow emotion to dictate to them in the decision-making process.

Even though many would argue against the fact that political correctness is a form of cultural Marxism, we need look no further than the most basic definition provided by Anthony Browne in his book *The Retreat of Reason*.

*"At its most fundamental, political correctness seeks to redistribute power from the powerful to the powerless. At its most crude, it opposes power for the sake of opposing power, making no moral distinction between whether the powerful exercise their power in a way that can be rationally and reasonably justified."*[86]

Therein lies not only the *problem* with political correctness, but the *connection* it has to Marxism itself. For political correctness to work and actually *redesign* society, it must be able to separate people and groups into "victims" and "aggressors." Anyone who is *not* perceived as a victim (or *in sympathy* with them) is seen as the *aggressor* in a battle *against* the victim. Those are the only two real categories of society that political correctness can and does recognize: *victims* and *aggressors*.

This is why the Left is so visceral in its condemnation of anyone who is *not* part of the Left. They believe they are fighting for the true victims in society against those on the Right, whom they classify as *aggressors*.

As Browne states, *"political correctness automatically supports the weak and vulnerable, classifying them as nearly untouchable victims, irrespective of whether they merit such support or not. When the successful, affluent, powerful Dutch film maker Theo van Gogh was ritually murdered in the streets of Amsterdam for insulting Islam, the politically correct, including the Guardian and Index on Censorship, automati-*

---

[86] Anthony Browne, The Retreat of Reason (2006), p. 9

*cally sided with the comparatively powerless Islamic Dutch-Moroccan killer."*[87]

The basis for deciding on a course of action as far as who to support is *not* based on *reason* or even *merit* but on emotion or virtue. For instance, anyone who is a capitalist is seen as the *aggressor* (regardless how many jobs they provide). This explains why people like Michael Moore are desperate to be seen as part of the victim group, in spite of the fact that his net worth of $50 million dollars obviously places him far above true victims.

As long as Michael Moore continues to portray himself as the victim of the capitalistic elite, he will continue to be seen as a victim. This is in spite of the truth that he is a capitalist who has amassed more money that most of us would realize in ten lifetimes. Since he is seen as a victim, he can say what he says against the "aggressors" and whether his words are true or not, they are accepted as true because of his victimhood status.

It used to surprise and anger me when the media would stop broadcasting some very important piece of news in favor of something else. This occurred, for instance, just as the issue of Benghazi was gaining momentum and it appeared that it might create problems for the Obama administration. But what happened? Hurricane Sandy hit the shore and devastated entire neighborhoods, leaving people without homes and the basic necessities in life. The media was able to switch gears from the Benghazi situation to focus almost entirely on Hurricane Sandy's devastation. This also allowed Mr. Obama – through various photo ops – to look like a leader. Was Hurricane Sandy important to cover? Of course, and the damage it caused still exists.

---

[87] Anthony Browne, The Retreat of Reason (2006), p. 10

But why was it covered to the exclusion of Benghazi? Obviously, it had to do with perceived victims, didn't it? Benghazi, at its root, is about a nearly-Third World country and the big "aggressor" of the United States. Yes, a handful of Americans were killed. So what? Why were we there anyway, many would ask? The attitude that you "get what you deserve" is the natural response of the politically correct after determining the victim from the aggressor.

So, it was easy for the media to begin focusing on victims of the weather and leave their coverage of Benghazi behind. After a number of days or a few weeks, things settled down and the media was then able to simply segue into focusing on other things and felt no obligation to return to the issue of Benghazi. They also stopped focusing on the effects of Hurricane Sandy, in spite of the fact that neighborhoods continued to exist under the devastation of the hurricane, supplies did not get where they were supposed to be, and in general, people continued to suffer for some time.

What the media could have and should have done was to focus on Hurricane Sandy while continuing coverage of Benghazi. However, even when Benghazi was being covered by the press, it wasn't being covered in an honest manner. Even though four Americans died in Benghazi, the Obama administration was seen as the real "victim" with the "aggressive" press (allegedly backed by the GOP) doing what it could to take down the administration. More than a few people claimed the whole attack on the Obama administration was nothing more than an attempt at political gain from the GOP. In the end, Benghazi, for many people, has nothing to do with right or wrong but how people feel about who is the real victim in the situation. For them, the GOP is the aggressor and the Obama administration is the victim; therefore, the Obama administration needs to be "protected." End of story.

This resolute need or insistence to support the victim while vociferously denouncing the aggressor is a staple of the politically correct system. *"Automatically opposing the powerful and supporting the powerless means that, when presented with a new issue, the politically correct must decide not what is right or wrong, malign or benign, true or untrue, but who is the more powerful and who the less powerful. The PC analytical process enjoys the beauty of simplicity:*

- *Identify the victim.*
- *Support them and their interests, irrespective of any other factors."*[88]

The idiocy of this belief system results in the fact, as Browne states, that *"victims are supported not because they are right but because they are vulnerable"*[89] and when anyone takes the time to apply critical analysis to the alleged victim's situation, they are quickly seen as the aggressor because of it, even if their analysis is right on the mark. This "aggression" toward victims is seen as oppression and must be opposed.

You see, this is one of the largest reasons why I have a difficulty with people on the Left who say they are Christian. If they support and align themselves with unwritten policy and code created by political correctness, they are not aligning themselves with truth at all. They are aligning themselves with something that merely appears to be truth, though as we have seen, it really bears no resemblance to truth – biblical truth. Therein lies the problem. Those who have bought into the politically correct movement wind up essentially ignoring the truth of Scripture. They do this because, within politically correct circles, truth is not based on reason, but on emotional virtue.

Ultimately, political correctness is predicated upon the false notion of how to determine the "victim" from the "aggressor." It is done through an emotional resonance within them, which translates to their truth.

---

[88] Anthony Browne, The Retreat of Reason (2006), p. 11
[89] Ibid, p. 13

As opposed to this, the Bible contains God's absolute truth and it is non-negotiable. We are to follow it whether our emotions go along with us or not. This is exactly what Jesus did. He followed the Father's truth to the core, regardless of how He may have felt about a situation. Look no further than the Garden of Gethesemane as a perfect illustration.

Emotions are difficult to live with and we tend to follow their dictates in spite of the lack of reason. Browne notes, *"One of the ironies of political correctness is that, since it subjugates objective truth to subjective virtue, it often causes more harm than good...the world is not short of good intentions, but it is too often short of good reasoning."*[90]

For instance, double standards exist as part of the fabric of society and are acceptable only if the "victims" gain from it. The double standard should always favor the victim, not the aggressor. It does not matter that those who are seen as "aggressors" are discriminated against because of it.

A woman is essentially given the right to abort the unborn child she carries and can do so without obtaining her partner's permission. Many would say that this is as it should be because a woman should have control over her own body. (A woman who is denied an abortion is the "victim" even though her intent is to victimize her unborn child. Political correctness, instead of being at odds with this truth, simply redefines things and the unborn child is declared "fetal tissue," which removes personhood.)

But consider the fact that a married man who opts for a vasectomy cannot obtain one unless he gains written consent from his wife. On one hand, society says that a woman has complete and final control over her body, even when she is carrying another human being. On the other hand, a man who simply wants to become clinically "ster-

---

[90] Anthony Browne, The Retreat of Reason (2006), p. 15

ile" so that he cannot father another child cannot do so without permission of his wife. This is a clearly a double standard that is acceptable in society because the man is seen as the "aggressor" while the woman is seen as the "victim." However, in this case, the man is victimized because of the double standard that is inherent in both situations, the abortion and the vasectomy.

Political correctness has really been around since the fall of humanity. It was clearly present in the Garden of Eden when the Tempter provided a relative version of "truth" that made both Eve and Adam feel as though they were somehow the "victims" against God, the "Aggressor."

Because of his ability to make our first two parents see themselves as "victims" of God's "lordship" (aggression), Satan successfully caused them to listen to and obey their emotion, which determined truth for them. Because of it, the fall occurred, and with it the unnatural desire to look to emotion as the arbiter of truth. This is political correctness. It believes the lie because it feels right, not because it is right.

This is the crux of the problem, the very heart of the issue. Political correctness is built on a lie, a lie that says truth is determined by the way our emotions react to something. God says He is Truth and if we learn from Him, we will come to understand that truth is not determined by our emotions. Absolute truth has everything to do with God's immutable standards.

As we progress toward the end of the age, more and more people in society will turn from those immutable standards to follow a path of relativism, which leads to spiritual ruin. They will do so gladly because they will thoroughly come to believe that they have found the far better way: truth determined by virtue. The end of that path, unfortunately, leads to hell. I pray you're not on it.

## Chapter 20
# The "Victim" and the "Aggressor"

W e have discussed the fact that the *oversimplification* of issues by those within the arena of political correctness (PC) causes them to divide everyone into two categories; either a person is a "victim" or they are the "aggressor." The "victim" is seen as being "right" (and *supported*) while the "aggressor" is understood to be "wrong" (and consequently *vilified*). It is as basic and as simplistic as that.

A person is determined to be a victim if he/she is up against someone or something that *appears* to be stronger. Strength represents aggression, regardless of whether or not it *is* that. It is *seen* as lording it over others and creating victims because of it. All "good" people then must fight against the aggressor. Those who defend "aggressors" become just as vilified.

For instance, the president of Planned Parenthood, Cecile Richards, can publicly announce that declaring a fetus a *human being* is an "extremist" position[91] and women's groups and supporters will agree with her. She is referring to the recent North Dakota *Personhood Amendment*. Richards notes, "*These politicians don't care about women or whether these matters are on the minds of the American people.*"[92]

This is exactly how the PC see issues in life and react to them. The absurdity of her words masks a political subterfuge. Richards and others like her must always bring it back to a focus on women and women's rights and do everything in their power to *eradicate* the fact that women who have abortions *are* carrying a human life within them. The focus cannot be on the unborn human being but on women's "health" issues, and it should stay there.

Richards claims that politicians do not care about women. She also denies that a fetus is a human being. As the representative for Planned Parenthood, she cannot admit that the unborn child *is* a human being because if she does, she immediately becomes a hypocrite *and* guilty of supporting murder. She *has* to deny that a fetus is a human being so that those who attack Planned Parenthood then are seen as solely attacking *women*.

---

[91] http://weaselzippers.us/2013/03/24/planned-parenthood-ceo-declaring-a-fetus-a-human-being-is-extremism/ (03/26/2013)
[92] Ibid

For the politically correct minions (including Planned Parenthood), a woman carries an unborn baby to term and delivers a baby. At *that* point *(after the birth)*, it magically *becomes* a human being. A woman who is pregnant with an unborn baby, but opts to *abort* (even as late as the third trimester through the partial-birth abortion method), kills something that is *never* seen as a human being. This is how political correctness works.

Remember, Richards *must* emphasize that women are the "victims" here by focusing on women's "health" issues. She does this by making a sweeping generalization that politicians do not "care" about women or their "health" issues. It's an untenable position, but it is done so that she forces the focal point of the discussion to remain on women as "victims" (without using the term), and this focus disregards the fact that an unborn child is in the mix. The people at Planned Parenthood can never waver from this position at all.

This is why a person who, for instance, shoots a pregnant woman during a robbery or carjacking is often charged with two *murders* (if both mother and unborn child die). The accepted assumption is that the mother had *every* intention of carrying the unborn child to full term and giving birth. In that case, the law sees the perpetrator as being a murderer of the unborn child as well as of the mother.

However, if the same woman had gone to an abortion clinic and *paid* to literally have the child *murdered*, this action is *acceptable* by law because the *woman* made the decision to end her unborn baby's life and abortion is not seen as murder. In that case, the unborn child is *never* recognized as a human being.

In both cases, the *murder* of an unborn baby *occurred*. Yet because one method (abortion) is socially acceptable (another term for *political correctness*), it is *not* considered murder. It is considered a legal "choice" by the mother and the doctor is merely paid to perform a "health" service that removes *fetal tissue* from the womb, regardless of the age or development of the "fetal tissue."

Those who claim to be *Christians* and see life through the lens of political correctness must look seriously at *how* they make their decisions. In nearly all situations, these individuals base their decisions *not* on *biblical truth* but on the ever-changing tapestry of *societal relativism*. If they would stop to consider the fact that they are actually aligning themselves with atheists, agnostics, and in general, people who are in complete *rebellion* toward God and His *absolute truth*, they might realize the problem.

God considers societal relativism (or political correctness) to be *compromising* with the world, regardless of how well-intentioned individuals may be who call themselves Christian. Far from standing on *His* truth, they are firmly in line with the *world's* relativism or "virtue."

So, even though God says *"thou shalt not kill,"* for instance, those who claim to be Christian yet use political correctness to define their position do so by setting God's immutable law aside, replacing it with human-made moral relativism. How is that Christian? We understand that when God issued that command, He was speaking of premeditated *murder* since He also made provision for those who accidentally killed someone or killed someone in self-defense (cf. Exodus 22:2-3; see also Nehemiah 4:17-18).

In the case of abortion, these individuals claiming to be Christian *choose* to believe that women are "victims," so their decision is made clear. It is to fight those whom they see as *oppressing* women (keeping them from having an abortion, in this case). This is in spite of the fact that the "aggressors" they fight against are also fighting *for* the rights of thousands of *unborn* babies every day: true innocents, who have no one to speak for them and whose innocent blood is spilled, something that God abhors (as the Scripture points out in places like Deuteronomy 19: 10; Proverbs 6:17; cf. 2 Kings 8:12; 15:16; Hosea 13:16; Amos 1:13).

To the politically correct "Christian," their truth is clearly (and only) seen in who is the "victim." Having arrived at that conclusion (in spite of God's absolute truth, which judges not based on victim/aggressor, but on the act of a person), that the unborn child is *not* the victim, but the woman *is*, they find ways to make God's Word fit into their preconceived idea of truth.

In all issues that face society, it is *imperative* for those within the politically correct camp to determine *victim* and *aggressor*. That is the starting point for them in determining "truth." Once this is accomplished, it is merely a matter of "aggressively" supporting the "victim" while also viscerally castigating those who are seen as standing against that "victim" (aka, the aggressors).

This is why – according to the politically correct – the Tea Party is evil. The Tea Party is seen as the *aggressor* because it supports capitalism, as well as the Constitution and Bill of Rights as the rule of law in America. Ultimately, the Tea Party believes in biblical values as outlined by the founders. This stance is anathema to the politically correct. This is one reason why people were and are so desperate to paint the Tea Party as *racist* and *sexist*, in spite of not one shred of evidence to prove the charges.

It is also why the Occupy Movement, which leaves tons of garbage and destruction in its wake, is seen as the *victim* because it is opposed to corporate America, or *capitalism*, which is seen as the aggressor. The Occupy Movement – the perceived *victim* – is given a wide berth to do what it needs to do by the politically correct (including the media) and among politicians. The Tea Party – the stated *aggressor* – is the enemy of "freedom" and "equality" and should, in every respect, be verbally abused by the media and virtually everyone else.

Another example of how political correctness works is seen in a recent discussion that occurred on Al Sharpton's show. In it, he and two others focused on Mayor Bloomberg of New York City and his continued efforts to abrogate the Second Amendment. Right out of the chute, the race card was played – anti-Semitism – because of Bloomberg's Jewish ethnicity.

> *"MIKE BARNICLE: Let's get down to it: Mike Bloomberg, Mayor of New York City. I mean, there's a level of anti-Semitism in this thing, directed toward Bloomberg –*
>
> *"AL SHARPTON: No doubt about it.*
>
> *"BARNICLE: I mean, it's out there.*
>
> *"DAN SENOR: I don't think it's anti-Semitism. I think it's the perception of big-city urban elites, wealthy elites, telling the rest of the little people how to live their lives.*
>
> *"SHARPTON: But if he were not a big-city Jewish man, in some parts I think it would be different."*[93]

The only one who sort of got it right was Dan Senor, though I believe he was off the mark as well. It is not so much *"big-city urban elites"* telling the rest of us how to live. It is the fact that Bloomberg believes the Second Amendment is outmoded and needs to be seriously curtailed or eradicated.

As for Sharpton's agreement that the attacks on Bloomberg are due to racism, this is the guy who invented the word! Tawana Brawley,

---

[93] http://newsbusters.org/blogs/mark-finkelstein/2013/03/25/sharpton-barnicle-agree-anti-semitism-explains-opposition-bloomber#ixzz2OYzGu3iL (03/26/2013)

Crown Heights, and so many other situations that Sharpton has inserted himself into and fanned into flame for personal gain are too numerous to mention here. He is a professional race-baiter, and yet he has no problem making racist statements against Jews when he feels he needs to do. *"If the Jews want to get it on, tell them to pin their yarmulkes back and come over to my house."*[94]

Sharpton is a complete ass, but since he is black, he is also seen as the "victim" at the hands of the white race (the "aggressor" in this case). Therefore, the media will gloss over (or ignore) anything that Sharpton says that can be construed as racist or simply wrong. So when Sharpton speaks racism against Jewish people, he is still seen as the "victim." He can also make statements in support of someone who is Jewish without being seen as duplicitous, depending on the specific issue at hand. Sharpton always speaks as a "victim" and therefore is never wrong, even when he actually *is* wrong.

Victims and aggressors. Determining who is and who is not is what it amounts to for the politically correct. In its over-simplistic reaction to the weighty issues of life, political correctness too often *circumvents* truth in favor of *emotional virtue* (humanistic relativism).

There is absolutely no room for *humanistic relativism* within Christianity, and those who say they *are* Christians but are deeply ensconced within the Left's camp are anti-God because they use another "truth" to determine their course of action. They do not use God's absolute truth, though they would argue they are doing just that.

Jesus *never* put up with the nonsense we call humanistic relativism, which guides most (if not *all*) politically correct situations. Humanistic relativism – based on *emotional virtue* – is diametrically opposed to God and His truth, which *never* changes.

---

[94] http://www.realclearpolitics.com/articles/2010/08/05/newsweek_whitewashes_al_sharpton_106619.html (03/26/2013)

Political correctness, on the other hand, forces new outlooks all the time, depending on the situation and who is defined as the "victim" and the "aggressor." This is done by using the ever-changing "truth" of relativism.

As far as God is concerned, all human beings are *aggressors*, willfully rebelling against Him and the absolute truth of His Word. It is our "emotional virtue" that causes us to take this stance. It began with Adam and Eve. They then embarked on a road that they were never intended to go down. Humanity has been walking down that path ever since.

Funny how we *always* manage to change the truth of God into a lie, and it's always for our own benefit. It would be so much easier if we simply *agreed* with God in the first place. Of course, that would require an uncompromising attitude of honesty toward God, wouldn't it?

# Chapter 21
# Only One Solution

157. Jesus Dies on the Cross
The Gospel According to St. John. Chapter 19, Verses 25–30.

I would be completely remiss if I ended this book without offering at least some kind of solution to the problems we face in this world. If you're *not* a Christian, then the solution I'm pointing out is outlined in the next chapter, which is also the final chapter of this book.

It has come to be the way I end all of my books. There is no more important decision each person can or will make than whether or not to receive the only true salvation that is available, the very salvation that Jesus Christ made possible for us. If you do not know Jesus, then please, I cannot urge you strongly enough, receive His salvation and enter into a life-changing relationship with Him. It means the difference between heaven and hell.

However, if you *are* an authentic Christian, then this chapter will hopefully end on a high note for you. What do we do as authentic Christians who are bound to face increasing erosion of our rights under the US Constitution and greater tyranny from our own government?

There really is only one answer of which I am aware. It is twofold in nature, but it is the answer that the Bible repeatedly gives us as the means to peace in our daily walk with God.

- *Submit to His will in all things*
- *Praise Him in the midst of all things*

Honestly, is there anything else a Christian *can* or *should* do? If we believe that God controls all outcomes and that everything that comes our way will eventually work out according to His will for our good and His glory, how can we *not* submit ourselves to Him and praise Him for all things?

**Difficulties of Life**

I will admit that this is very difficult for me. In essence, it is the very substance of what being a Christian means. I like being in control as much as possible. When I consider what is ahead of us, I *do* become somewhat nervous and apprehensive. Will the government be able to successfully remove our guns from society? If so, what will that mean for me and my ability to protect my family from home invasions, for instance?

Is the Lord protecting me anyway? If so, should I not be casting all my cares on Him because He cares for me? That's what Peter tells us in 1 Peter 5:7. But then Paul tells us that the man who does not care for his own household is worse than an infidel (cf. 1 Timothy 5:8). That means quite a bit in reality, from things like providing food and a roof overhead to issues that revolve around safety. What do I do? How about if work becomes so difficult that we lose our jobs?

All of these things and more are the things that concern me. Some would say I'm borrowing trouble that may never come. Others would say that I should not be concerned about those things *until* they come.

The truth is that we live in a world that is constantly changing and becoming even more evil. We have talked about these things throughout these pages. Yet in spite of everything, God is fully in control of all outcomes. If we are His – as the Bible assures us we are through faith in the finished work of Christ – then will He not provide? Will He not take care of us?

**Can We Trust God or Not?**
The only and obvious answer is that He *will*. In the here and now, I can and should *prepare* for coming hardships. I should do what I can to have things in my pantry and storehouse that will keep us going for up to three months – more if I can swing it. It is important that each person do what they can in order to *not* have to depend upon the government or others when the bottom falls out.

At the same time, we make these preparations knowing that God watches over us and cares for us. We do not know what will happen tomorrow. We do not know how far into the future total financial collapse may be. We do not know when the Rapture will occur, nor do we know when the Tribulation will begin.

Until these things occur, we also do not know how bad things will become for the average person, do we? There really is no way to know.

I believe there are many portions of Scripture that speak to the need to trust Him and let Him deal with the problems that He allows to come into our lives. Let me close this chapter by focusing on wisdom from one of the Psalms. Memorize this. Take it with you in your heart wherever you go. Learn to let it speak to you as you contemplate the problems that face your life.

The only solution to any problem we face is *God*. The only solution to any nervousness, fear, or trepidation we experience is *God*. The only solution for whatever comes into our life that brings with it sorrow, tragedy, or abysmal problems are with God. He and He alone is the answer.

It is up to us to submit these problems and difficulties to Him until we can freely and completely release them into His care. That is a must, and it truly separates those who merely say they are Christians from those who actually are Christians.

### Psalm 100

*Shout joyfully to the Lord, all the earth.*

*Serve the Lord with gladness;*

*Come before Him with joyful singing.*

*Know that the Lord Himself is God;*

*It is He who has made us, and not we ourselves;*

*We are His people and the sheep of His pasture.*

*Enter His gates with thanksgiving*

*And His courts with praise.*

*Give thanks to Him, bless His name.*

*For the Lord is good;*

*His lovingkindness is everlasting*

*And His faithfulness to all generations.*

This is what we are to do. We are to first of all *shout,* and we are to shout with joy *to* the Lord. The Psalmist is literally commanding everything on the earth to call out to God with *praise*. That should be our first and continuous order of business.

Paul emphasizes this as well when he says that we should praise God in *all* things (cf. 1 Thessalonians 5:18). In doing so, we are recognizing that God is *in charge* of our lives.

But some might say, *"That is very difficult to believe!"* Yes, I know it is, but because we have a challenging time believing in something does not mean that we give up trying to believe it. It means that we have to persevere that much more until that fear turns to belief and belief turns to knowledge.

We should praise God in all things. Difficult, but it must be done if we are to exercise faith in God and His control over our lives.

Next, we should *serve* the Lord, and we should do this how? We should serve Him with *gladness*. That again is often very difficult, but there is only one solution to our doubts: *perseverance*. We cannot give up here. We must continuously praise God with everything that is within us so that we will find ourselves emotionally removed from the circumstances that wish to bind us in fear.

The Psalmist then goes on to say that our lives should be filled with joyful singing and we should come to recognize that God is our *Lord*. He is our Shepherd, and like the loving and careful shepherd who takes care of *all* the sheep in His care, God will surely do the same thing with us.

Since we are the sheep of *His* pasture, it is logical then to assume that He is the One who provides for us. His eye is always on us, our troubles, and our lives in general. He does not forget us and is always mindful of our frailties.

The Psalmist then reminds us that God is *good*. He is far more than good, but this one word helps us understand that *because* of the fact that He is good, He will do what is best for us. He is not some evil being bent on teasing us unmercifully until we bend to His deceitful will!

God has only our best interests in His heart and seeks to bring those to fruition every day. The Psalmist ends with two declarations. God's lovingkindness will never fail because it is eternal, and He is faithful to authentic Christians in *every* generation. These are two truths upon which Christians stand. We must never forget them. We must always be aware of them and we must allow these truths to penetrate our hearts and lives in order that He will be glorified in and through us.

God is not going to leave us, and when we are tempted to think that He has or will, we need to remind ourselves of the truth of Scripture. Romans 8 tells us He will never leave or forsake us and that because we are in Christ, not only are we not on the receiving end of God's condemnation, but we will *never* be on the receiving end of it!

God is good. His goodness lasts forever and it is always directed toward those who are part of His family – those who are in relationship to Jesus Christ.

The only solution that I am aware of related to the problems this life throws at us is found in submitting our will to God and praising Him in all things. Try as I might, I have found no other Scriptural remedy for life's problems, and even though I do not live these things perfectly, God always brings me back to them.

My prayer for you is that He will do the same thing for you so that your life will be filled with His peace, you will learn to trust Him in all things, and you will be freed to fulfill the Great Commission. May He be praised forever.

## Chapter 22
# Looking Ahead

D o you know *when* you will die? Are you aware of the *day* and *hour* when you will slip from this life into eternity? I'm betting you are not privy to that information. So why are you living as if you **_do_** *know when it will happen?* Putting a decision about Jesus off until another day is taking a huge chance because of the fact that you do not know when you will die. That is plainly simple, and logic alone demands that you do not put this decision off. Yet you do, because the thought of becoming a Christian makes you feel uncomfortable.

You wrongly believe that to become a Christian means that you have to change in a major way *before* Jesus will accept you. It means to you giving up the things you love now because if you love them, then obviously they are wrong and God does not love them.

You are putting the cart before the horse. You must understand that God is not rejecting you. He is not standing there, tapping His foot, demanding that you eliminate those things that He does not like before you can come to Him for salvation.

If you (or anyone) could do that, you would not *need* His salvation at all. It is because you and I do things that are not pleasing to Him that we need His salvation.

What do you do that you would like to no longer do? Do you drink excessively until you cannot control it? Do you play around with drugs? Do you eat too much food until you have become overweight, lethargic and sickly?

What other things are in your life that you do not like? Are you drawn to illicit extra-marital affairs? Do you have a problem with lust? Are you a shopaholic? Do you tend to tell lies a great deal because it makes you feel important, or to hide things about your life?

Do you find that you do not like people and you would prefer to be around animals or out in the woods than around people? Are you a workaholic? Do you place a high value on money and you find that you work very hard to obtain it?

Here's the problem. The enemy of our souls comes to us and tells us that God will never accept us until we get rid of those things. He lies to us that God essentially wants us "perfect" before He will be willing to meet us and grant us eternal life. This is completely untrue.

The other lie that our enemy tells us is that we should not become a Christian because the fun in our life will fly out the door. We will no longer be able to drink or do the fun things we enjoy now. We start to think that coming to God means becoming a doormat for people and having to fill our life with things we do not want to *ever* do.

These are all lies, and unfortunately, too many people believe them. First of all, God does not expect you to be "perfect" before you come to Him for salvation. If that were the case, no one would be able to ever approach Him.

Secondly, God does not say that He is going to take away all the things we enjoy and replace them with things we hate. What is wrong with enjoying the lake on your boat? What is wrong with spending a day with the family fishing or just relaxing in the mountains? There is nothing wrong with these things.

What God *will* do is begin to remove the things that have ensnared you so that life is actually draining from you, but you are not aware of it. For instance, maybe you drink excessively and you have tried everything you can think of to quit. You have gone to AA meetings, spent thousands of dollars on this program or that, and you have even used your own will power to free yourself from the addiction to alcohol, all to no avail.

The question is not: *do I need to quit before I come to Jesus*? The question is: *am I willing to allow Him to work in and through me to take away the addiction I have to alcohol*? Do you see the difference? Are you willing to allow Him to work in you to break that addiction so that you will become a healthier person, one who is able to think straight and one who learns to rely on Him for strength? That is all He wants you to be able to do. He knows you cannot break that addiction (or any addiction for that matter) with your own strength and willpower. Are you willing to allow Him to do it in and through you?

What if you are a workaholic? What if you have "things" like a boat, a house in Cancun, a large bank account, four cars, and more? Do you think that God is going to ask you to give it up, or worse, do you think that God will simply come in and take all of that from you? I know of nothing in Scripture that tells us He will do that.

What God will do with all of those who come to Him trusting Him for salvation is one thing, which begins the moment we receive salvation and will continue until the day we stand before Him. He will begin to create within us the character of Jesus (cf. Ephesians 2:10).

Here is a verse from the Old Testament that was said originally through the prophet Ezekiel to the people of Israel. While this was specifically stated to the Jews, it is applicable to all who receive salvation through Jesus Christ.

*"I will give you a new heart and put a new spirit within you; I will take the heart of stone out of your flesh and give you a heart of flesh. I will put My Spirit within you and cause you to walk in My statutes, and you will keep My judgments and do them"* (Ezekiel 36:26-27).

God is speaking here through Ezekiel, and He is saying that He will give the people a new heart of flesh, removing that old heart of stone. This is God's responsibility. God is the One who makes that happen. We are told in the book of Hebrews that God is the Author and Finisher of our faith (cf. Hebrews 12:2). This tells me that God is the One who changes me from within so that over time, my desires are slowly turned into His desires.

I recall years ago thinking that God wanted to do everything in my life that I did not want Him to do. I fell into the asinine belief that He wanted to change everything about me. What I learned is that yes, there are things that God does want to change about me. However, there is a lot that God originally gave me that He has also enhanced and used for His glory.

Maybe you are a workaholic who thinks that working hard is something God does not want you to do. This is not necessarily the case.

He may have given you the ability and the knowledge to work in the area of finance for a great purpose. All He may wind up doing is dialing back your workaholic tendencies so that you have more time to enjoy your family and study His Word.

But you say you smoke, or drink, or use illegal drugs, and you don't want to give those up. As I stated, you can't give those up under your own power, and the fact that you have tried so many times has proven it to you.

But God knows what is and what is not good for you. Are you willing to *allow* Him to work in you to change your desires so that you no longer want to smoke, use illegal drugs, or drink nearly as much?

Then you say that you believe God wants to make you a Christian so you can become miserable. Isn't that what most Christians are – miserable? Not the Christians I know, and certainly not me, my wife, or our children.

Where does the Bible say that God wants us miserable? You will not find it. What God wants is for us to be blessed, and that begins when we receive salvation from His hand.

You know, if we would stop and take the time to consider the fact that this life is exceedingly short if we compare it to eternity, we will then realize that there is nothing so important that it should keep us from receiving Jesus as Savior and Lord.

Unfortunately, too many people do not consider the brevity of life. They think they will live forever, or at the very least, they will die when they are really old and gray. That will come too soon. Even though I have just recently turned 54, it still truly seems like yesterday that I was a young boy fishing in the Delaware River near Hobart, New York. There I spent many Saturdays fishing and simply enjoying being outdoors. How did life go by so very quickly? How could that have happened?

It has happened, and I am at a point in life where not only do I realize that this life is short, but I actually look forward to spending eternity with Jesus after this life. Does that sound morbid to you? It shouldn't, because by comparing this life to eternity, we should get a sense of what is truly important.

God does not expect us to become Mother Theresas. He does not necessarily expect us to give up everything and become missionaries in outer Mongolia. What God expects is for us to simply allow Him to change our character as He sees fit.

Over time, we may well find that we have simply stopped swearing without realizing it. Our desire for cigarettes or alcohol has nearly evaporated. Illicit affairs no longer enter the picture.

We also may find that some of the things we want to eliminate in our life become more pronounced. Often the enemy will do this to cause us to focus on something that God is not even doing in our lives at that point. It causes tension, frustration, and self-anger.

If you have gotten to this point in your life and you have not dealt with the question about Jesus, it is about time you do so. You need to stop what you are doing and realize a couple of things before you go through another minute in this life.

- **Sinner**: you need to realize that you are a sinner. You have sinned and you will continue to sin. Sin is breaking the laws that God has set up. We all sin. We have all broken God's laws and that breaks any connection we might have had with God. Sin pushes us away from Him.

  Romans 3:23 says, *"For all have sinned, and come short of the glory of God."* That means you and that means me. All means all. That is the first step. We need to recognize and agree with God that yes, we are sinners. I'm a sinner. You are a sinner. This results in God's anger, what the Bible terms "wrath."

- **God's Wrath**: Romans 1:18 says, *"For the wrath of God is revealed from heaven against all ungodliness and unrighteousness of men, who suppress the truth in unrighteousness."*

This is as much a fact as the truth that we are all sinners. Because we are sinners – by breaking God's law(s) – God has every right to be angry with us and ultimately destroy that which is sinful. If we choose to remain "in" our sinful states throughout this life, we will – unfortunately – be destroyed with the rest of sin.

Fortunately, there *is* a remedy, and it is salvation.

- **God's Gift**: In the sixteenth chapter of Acts, a jailer asks Paul this famous question: *what must I do to be saved?* The question was asked because Paul and Barnabas had been imprisoned, and while there, they began singing praises to God.

God then sent a powerful earthquake that opened the doors to all the prison cells, yet no one escaped. When the jailer arrived, he saw that everyone was still in their cells, and after seeing that miracle (what prisoner would not want to escape from prison?), turned and asked what he must do to be saved. He was speaking of the spiritual aspect of things. He wanted to know how he could be guaranteed eternal life.

The answer Paul gave the man was, *"Believe on the Lord Jesus Christ, and thou shalt be saved, and thy house"* (Acts 16:31).

This is not head knowledge or intellectual assent. This is *believing from the heart.* In fact, Paul makes a very similar statement in another book he wrote, Romans. He says, *"That if thou shalt confess with thy mouth the Lord Jesus, and shalt believe in thine heart that God hath raised him from the dead, thou shalt be saved. For with the heart man believeth unto righteousness; and with the mouth confession is made unto salvation"* (Romans 10:9-10).

When we fully believe something, we confess that it is true. It must begin in the heart because that is where the will is located. We must want to believe. We must endeavor to believe. We must seek to believe.

We must stop giving ourselves all the reasons to deny or ignore Jesus. As God, He became a Man, born of a virgin. He clothed Himself with humanity that He might show us how to live, and in so doing, would keep every portion of the law.

If Jesus was capable of keeping every portion of the law, then He would be found worthy to become a sacrifice for our sin – yours and mine. If He became a sacrifice for our sin, then all that we must do is embrace Him and His sacrificial death.

In short then, to become saved we must:

1. Admit (we sin)
2. Repent (want to turn away from it)
3. Believe (that Jesus is the answer)
4. Embrace (the truth about Jesus)

We **admit** that we are sinner, that we have sinned. This is nothing more than agreeing with God that we have broken His law. Can you honestly say that you have not broken God's law? If you admit to breaking even the "smallest" law, then you are a lawbreaker.

After we admit that we have sinned, the next step is found in **repenting**. Some believe that repenting is actually moving away from sin. This author believes that it is a willingness to move away from sin, and there is a difference.

As we have already discussed, it is impossible to stop sinning. Human beings simply cannot do it because as long as we live, we will have a sin nature, which is something within us that gives us a propensity to sin. As long as we have this inner propensity to sin or break God's laws, we will never be perfect in this life.

We cannot one day say, "Lord, I promise to stop sinning." If we do that, we are only kidding ourselves and setting ourselves up for major failure. We cannot stop sinning in this life. The most we can do is *want* to stop sinning and then spend the rest of our lives allowing God to create the character of Jesus within us, slowly, little by little.

Repenting is to decide that you no longer want to do the things that keep us out of heaven. We no longer wish to break God's laws. It is not promising God that we will never sin again.

Once we admit, then repent, we must **believe**. This is one of the most difficult things to do because believing that Jesus died in our place, that He lived a perfectly sinless life, is extremely difficult to believe. Our minds cannot grasp that truth. We must ask God to open our eyes to that truth so that we can embrace it.

While on the cross next to Jesus, the one thief joined the other thief in ridiculing Jesus. Then, all of a sudden – as we read in Luke 23 – this same thief that had just been ridiculing Him now turned to Him with a new understanding.

It was this new understanding that prompted the thief to say to Jesus, "*Lord, remember me when you come into your Kingdom.*" Jesus looked at the man and responded to him, "*Today, you will be with me in paradise.*"

What had occurred in the mind and heart of that thief from one moment to the next? One thing, and that one thing was that God opened the thief's eyes so that he could see the truth. It was as if the blinders fell off and he now saw and understood who Jesus was, even to the most cursory degree that Jesus was dying not for Himself, but for others.

It was this understanding, this awareness, which prompted the man to ask Jesus to simply be remembered. Jesus went way beyond it to promise the man that he would be with Jesus that day in paradise.

Please notice in Luke 23 that there is nothing in the chapter that tells us that the man promised Jesus he would give up sin, or that he would never sin again. There is nothing that tells us that thief took the time to enter into a final deathbed confession of his sins so that he could be absolved.

The thief made no promises to Jesus at all. What he experienced was the truth of who Jesus was and what Jesus accomplished for humanity. Jesus accomplished what we cannot. What is left is for each person to *admit, repent, believe,* and *embrace.*

Let me clarify here that though we do not see any verbal repentance from the thief, we know that he did repent. He admitted as well. How can we know this? It is simply due to the thief's complete about-face with respect to his attitude toward Jesus. One minute, he was ridiculing Jesus, and the next, embracing Him. This is important. There is no way he could have or would have *embraced* Jesus had he not been humbled by the truth *about* Jesus.

Once the thief saw the truth, he was instantly humbled. Within himself, he knew that he was a sinner, and in fact the text states that this is what he told the other thief dying next to him. *"But the other answering rebuked him, saying, Dost not thou fear God, seeing thou art in the same condemnation? And we indeed justly; for we receive the due reward of our deeds: but this man hath done nothing amiss*" (Luke 23:40-41). Something happened within the heart of the one thief. In one moment, the thief went from harassing Jesus to recognizing his own sinfulness and then ultimately asking for grace, which was freely given to him.

Whether he said it or not, the thief went from haughtiness to humility in a very short space of time, and it was all because he saw the truth about Jesus. That truth helped him realize that he deserved his death and what would happen to him after death. He understood that Jesus did not deserve death.

From here, the thief fully embraced the truth about Jesus and was rewarded with eternal life because of it. He did not come off the cross to be water baptized. He did not list a long litany of offenses against God. He recognized the truth about Jesus, was humbled, and embraced that truth!

This is what each of us needs to do. We cannot give in to the lie that tells us that we are not good enough, or we have not given up enough before God will accept us. We must reject the lie that says we must somehow earn our salvation.

Jesus has done everything that is necessary to make salvation available to us. The only thing that is left for us is to see the truth. Once we see that truth, it should humble us to the point of embracing Jesus and all that He stands for and is to us.

The eighth chapter of Romans begins with the fact that all who trust Jesus for salvation are no longer condemned...*ever*. All of my sins – past, present, and future – have not only been forgiven, but canceled. It is because of my faith in the atonement (death) of Jesus that God is able to cancel all of my sins, even the ones that I have not committed yet. This does not make me eager to commit them. It makes me want to do what I can to avoid sinning.

If you do not know Jesus, please do not put down this book without deliberately *believing* that He is God, that He died for you by the shedding of His blood on the cross, and that He rose three days later because death could not keep Him. Do you believe that? If you do not yet believe it, do you *want* to believe it? If so, then simply ask God to help you come to believe all that Jesus is and all that He has accomplished for you. God will answer your prayers and you may either receive instantaneous awareness of all that Jesus is and has done, or it may be a *growing* awareness over time. In either case, it is the most important decision you will ever make.

Turn to Him now and pray for knowledge of the truth and an ability to embrace it. Please. He is waiting for you.

## *Ask Yourself*:

1. Do you *know* Jesus? Are you in *relationship* with Him? Have you had a spiritual transaction according to John 3?
2. Do you *want* to receive eternal life through the only salvation that is available?
3. Do you believe that Jesus is God the Son, who was born of a virgin, lived a sinless life, died a bloody and gruesome death to pay for your sin, was buried, and rose again on the third day? Do you *believe* this?
4. Do you *want* to *embrace* the truth from #3?
5. Pray that God will open your eyes and provide you with the faith to begin believing the truth about Jesus. Ask Him to help your faith embrace the truth, realizing that you are not good enough to save yourself and that your sin will keep you out of God's Kingdom without His salvation.
6. Pray as if your life depended upon it because *it does*!
7. If you have prayed to receive Jesus as Savior and Lord, please write to me. I want to send you some materials at *no charge or obligation*. Write to me at **fred_deruvo@hotmail.com** and sign up for our free bimonthly newsletter at **www.studygrowknow.com**

*Falling Away*

Stop by our Internet page...http://studygrowknow.com

And check out our books...**FREE** to download.

www.ingramcontent.com/pod-product-compliance
Lightning Source LLC
LaVergne TN
LVHW081353060426
835510LV00013B/1795